Do you feel frantic and harried?

Do you ever sigh and say, "If only I had more time . . ."

Do you plan your days down to the last second—with no payoff in satisfaction?

Here is a unique step-by-step workshop approach that shows you how to break the frenzied cycle of your life. In an easy, informative, and amusing way

GET IT ALL DONE AND STILL BE HUMAN

will help you manage your time, decide what's important to you, and, in the process, improve the quality of your live.

GET IT ALL DONE AND STILL BE HUMAN

A PERSONAL TIME-MANAGEMENT WORKSHOP

TONY AND ROBBIE FANNING

BALLANTINE BOOKS · NEW YORK

Library of Congress Catalog Card Number: 78-14633

ISBN 0-345-34527-4

This edition published by arrangement with
Chilton Book Company

First Ballantine Books Edition: July 1980
Fourth Printing: July 1987

*To Mark Twain, who really understood
the evil effect Ben Franklin had on our lives*

Contents

Preface

Why is it that a decent person like you, someone you'd invite home for dinner, is plagued by the feeling that you'll never get it all done? When you aren't sighing, "If I only had more time . . . ," you're apologizing, "I've got to get it all together."

Do you think you invented Frantic?

You're not alone; there are millions like you, feeling harried and fractured. Guess what? It's not *all* your fault; there are real, not imagined, reasons, only some of which are under our control, why we all share this feeling of time scarcity.

But there are tricks you can learn to help you get it all done and still be human.

The modest aim of this book is to help you be a little easier on yourself. This is a private, personal, do-it-for-yourself workshop approach to helping you manage your personal time better so that you can improve the quality of your life. We've organized the book in as nontime-consuming a way as possible, so you can first, do something to break the cycle of hurry and frenzy, and begin to feel better about yourself; then use whatever tricks you need to keep the cycle from reestablishing itself; and only then, try to put your personal experience into a larger perspective.

We cannot be "time-management experts" for you, nor do we want to be. After all, the objective of managing one's time is to get on with the Good Life (whatever that is for you), and time-management should never be taken as a goal in itself. Ultimately, you're the only one who can be the time management expert for your life. But it helps to learn from others, so we've included examples from the experiences of our own lives, as well as those of our friends and students.

Many people start our workshops saying, "My personal life's in order—it's my work life I'd like to organize." Most of these leave with the realization that they were dead wrong on both counts and that, in fact, there is no wall between work time and personal time. Personal time is all we have.

Just remember, as you become your own personal time-management expert, that your life is not a series of little boxes to be checked off as you complete tasks. Life is rough, sweet, sticky, hot and cold, even messy. And enjoyable. There's no time-management system that can handle all that. So don't try to freeze the simple tricks you learn in this book into a rigid system. You deserve better of yourself.

Tony and Robbie Fanning
Menlo Park, California

Acknowledgments

Thanks to Lydia M. Driscoll and Kathryn Conover, our editors, and Elyse Sommer, our agent; Cate Keller for standing by the day we left for our cross-country bike trip; Janie Warnick, for introducing us to Tony Buzan's *Use Both Sides of Your Brain,* from which we learned the patterning technique; and Steve Sokolow, whose seminars in Creative Procrastination have been an inspiration to us.

Part One

ACTION

How to use Part One

You've got more than enough problems finding time for everything right now; so this part is not meant to be another drain on your time. Read it in little sessions, and each time read only as much as you can act on. Please *act* on each step in Part One: Action. Follow the step-by-step directions. It will take you very little time and it will personalize the rest of the book for you. People who have done this are surprised how little time it takes, but you shouldn't be. The subject is something you know the most about and are most interested in: yourself.

Before you go further

Part One: Action consists of four small steps. Half can be completed in your first twenty-minute period, half at another time or another day in a second twenty-minute period.

Stop. Free twenty minutes for yourself. Go to a private place where you can write. Take some sheets of paper, this book, and pens or pencils. You don't need to be alone for privacy; you just don't want someone peeking over your shoulder. Some private places in the midst of noise: the bathroom at home or at work, your car, the public library, a park, your bed (call in sick; then take the phone off the hook), the zoo, cafeterias.

Step One:
Lay Out a Big Picture

In order to rearrange your life to get what you want done, you need a clear picture of your life as it is today. Here is a simple and surprisingly fast way to lay out that picture in a very compact form.

The object is to put your life—all of it—on one sheet of paper. Then you can scan it at a glance.

1. In the center of a blank piece of paper, write the word "Life" and draw a circle around it:

Think of the many roles you play each day. As they occur to you, print them on spokes radiating from the center. These roles name the different faces we wear each day, and our relationships with other people and the outside world: father, mother, child, lover, businessperson, friend, runner, shopper, cook, artist, writer, student, teacher. What are the most important roles in your life? *No one else is going to see this,* so put down whatever is important to you.

You can turn the paper around when you write.

Comments

- Turn this pattern into a porcupine of roles. Print, so you can read this pattern more easily. This is a pattern, not an outline. No one is looking over your shoulder, even if you can hear the voice of your sixth-grade teacher telling you to line things up. Write as little as you need to, leaving room for more.
- To help identify all these facets of your life, think about how you spent yesterday; think of holidays, weekends, work days.
- Do it as quickly as you can, as each new role suggests itself, jot down one or two words. Very quickly, most of the important roles of your life will add themselves to the pattern. You can always come back and add more.

2. Once you are satisfied that your major roles are in

the pattern, branch out from the roles. Start by naming the persons or objects connected with the role, or by naming the activities involved in those roles—whatever pops into your mind. Keep branching away from the center. The more you list, the more you'll think of. If you think of another role, put another spoke from the center. When an activity pops into your mind, insert it as another branch. By the time you're done, the whole pattern will be ringed with activities.

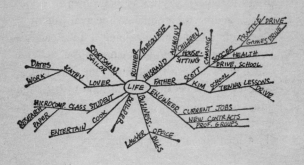

Are you done? Don't read any more until you've finished your own Life pattern. When you are satisfied with it, you are done for now.

Comments

- Patterning (which is what you're doing) is just another way of organizing your thoughts. There is nothing magical about patterning: it is merely useful—and fast. It does seem to mirror the way the human mind works.
- Don't analyze!
- Is it easy or hard for you? You may start slowly at

first, until you begin to concentrate on the thoughts flashing through your brain. Then the ideas come so fast and thick, you'll barely be able to write them fast enough.

- Turn your paper around when necessary; the pattern will quickly begin to bristle with branches.
- Don't hesitate to start over, if you run out of room. If your life is complex, write smaller the second time or use a bigger piece of paper (or tape two pieces together). Try not to bog down in details. You're aiming for a broad and general pattern.
- This patterning technique-doing a Life pattern— externalizes the way you worry. The activities which show up can't help being the ones that are closest to you, because this method of patterning brings out, via association, the most urgent and important activities.
- Do it for right now, not for the past.

PATTERNING

The patterning technique we're using is based on the way your brain generates ideas. You can think of it as a fancy way of outlining, but it isn't. Remember in grade school how they taught you to study by making an outline of your subject?

I. THE PAST
A. When: 87 years ago
B. Who: our ancestors
C. What: started a new country
1. Liberty

2. Everyone equal

II. NOW

The trouble with outlines is that they're only good for analyzing something that's already done. You can't outline something you're creating until you're done creating. Outlining breaks down; patterning builds up. Patterning mirrors the way your brain creates ideas. The whole point of patterning is to capture information and ideas as they're generated without trying to organize them first. Applying patterning to your life allows you to see all the facets without first bogging down in setting priorities or making plans for what you want to do. It's also hard to moralize in a pattern but depressingly easy in an outline. All this explains why it's so easy to get the hang of patterning.

Patterns are as unique as fingerprints. Each Life pattern, however, is only interesting to the person who drew it. In fact, it's annoying to look at someone else's Life pattern.

For this reason we won't clutter this book and your brain with more examples of other people's Life patterns. Unless you saw the pattern grow before your eyes, and unless you knew that person well, you wouldn't understand their thinking pattern, just as they wouldn't understand yours.

This patterning technique, incidentally, is useful anytime you want to examine information: what's discussed at meetings, something you're studying (kids quickly take to the patterning technique), lists of errands.

It is an effective, fast way to gather and externalize your thoughts.

3. In your Life pattern, you have created an overall view of your life as it is today, with all its important facets. But some things are missing. Nagging away in that small un-

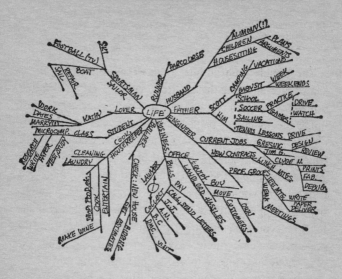

comfortable corner at the back of your mind are all those things you've started: your wishes and regrets.

Now is the time to sort them out. What is missing from your life? What, exactly, are you not doing that you wish you were doing or had done? Put it in your Wish list (regrets are only wishes about the past). Like your Life pattern, this will be for your eyes only, so be honest with yourself.

Before you write out your own wishes and regrets, look at some of the more mundane ones others have wished.

WISH LIST

Unfinished	Unstarted
remodel kitchen	weight lifting
sewing pile	wandering, time alone
disorganized workbench	sewing for myself
garage	ride bike across United States
make birthday present for Mom	help at school, kids' groups, library
finish my degree	

repair windows
plans for vacation
gardening
run every day
tennis lessons
hang rope swing for kids

write/answer letters
learn serigraphy
take business class
spend time with kids
meet new people
read for pleasure
painting, drawing, pottery
sail around the world
yoga
diet
start a journal

Now *you* do it. Write your Wish list. Set aside another twenty minutes, find a retreat, and on a blank piece of paper or at the bottom of your Life pattern, write:

WISH LIST

Unfinished   *Unstarted*

and start listing. Don't go any further until your Wish list is completed.

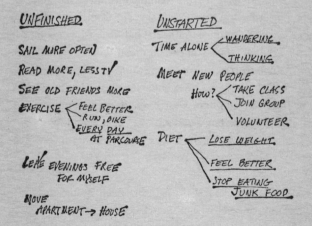

Comments

- Don't think that all unfinished activities are chore-type ones, or that all unstarted ones must be creative ones. When you make your Wish list, if you're not getting it done and it bothers you, list it. Don't worry about how trivial it seems. List it; it's for your eyes only. If you feel bad about not using dental floss every day, list it. The purpose of this exercise is to expose the nagging voices. Later, you can still them.

- Some people have trouble with the unfinished half. They can't think of items to put on it. A helpful viewpoint is that nothing is finished unless you're satisfied with it. So if you built a rocking horse for your kids and they've been using it for a couple of years, but it bothers you that the face hasn't been painted—that's unfinished, for you. List it.

- If you have trouble with the unstarted half, remember the last time you thought, "Gee, that looks like fun!" If you're not that kind of person, remember the last time you turned green with envy at someone who was doing something you weren't.

- Definitely put in your fantasies. But be honest about your fantasies, even if they're illegal, immoral, or fattening. Almost every item in the sample list was a fantasy at the time for the person who contributed it.

4. Look at your Life pattern. Each of the unfinished/unstarted regrets/wishes you listed in your Wish list fits into it somewhere. You may already have put it into your Life pattern. Add everything you listed under Unfinished

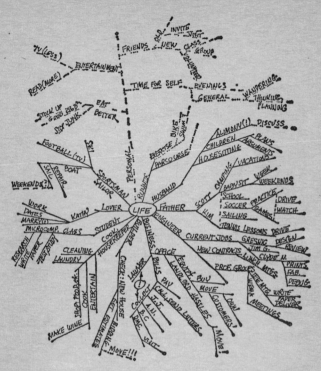

and Unstarted to the branches of your Life pattern. (It might help if you wrote these additions in a different color, or on a dotted line.)

If you cannot find a category for something on your Wish list, you need to create a new branch off of your Life expressly for that particular item. Often people spend all their time doing for others and not for themselves. We all need a "personal" or "just for me" branch. Is that what's missing from your Life pattern? Add it, if it is.

You have now completed the four smaller parts of Step

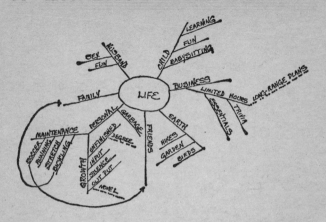

One and you have a visual picture of who you are today and what you would like to add to your life.

Make sure you keep your Wish list. You'll use if again, soon. Fold it and stash it into the back of this book.

Before you start reading step two

STOP. You need another twenty minutes, so free it for yourself. You will need privacy again, even more so than when you were drawing up your Life pattern. You will need a piece of paper and pens or pencils.

Step Two: List Uppers
and Downers

Now we come to the most personal step. You will draw up another, much simpler, pattern that you probably won't want anyone else to see. So far you've focused in on and laid out your activities via your Life pattern. The object of that brief exercise was to get it out onto paper and to see your life as a larger picture. The next pattern will express nothing more than how much you *like* what you're doing. Once again, nothing is sacred about this pattern—it's useful, that's all.

Turn a sheet of paper sideways (you'll see why in a moment) and divide it up like this:

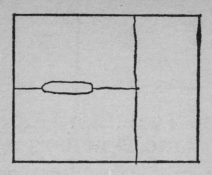

Now pick a time interval—yesterday, last week, last month—which is representative of your life. What's "representative"? If you spent the last two weeks on vacation in Hawaii, it's probably not representative, so pick some other period. If you worked all seven days last week, sixteen hours a day-and you normally don't—pick some other period.

A simple rule-of-thumb for picking your representative period: look at your Life pattern, at the ring of *roles*. If you played most of these roles during your chosen period, it's a representative one.

On your paper, write in that representative period.

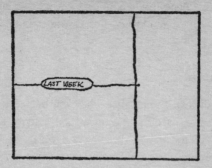

Now make a pattern of all the activities you can remember for that period, according to whether you liked doing them or not.

1. Above the line, list activities you distinctly remember liking, or neutral activities which you neither liked nor disliked. These are "Uppers."

2. Below the line, list activities you remember with displeasure. These are "Downers."

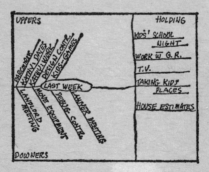

3. We're all complex, and so are many of our activities. The ones which you can't decide about, ones toward which you feel ambivalent, can be listed on the right-hand side—

the Holding Zone. Eventually most of these can be broken
down and sorted into Uppers and Downers, but don't bother
with that yet.

Comments

- If you can't remember what you did yesterday—
  it's all a haze of movement and activity and too
  difficult to sort out—keep track of today. From time
  to time add to the Upper/Downer pattern what's
  been happening to you. Do it soon, after it actually
  happens.
- Gut reactions while listing are easiest to classify
  into Uppers and Downers, but activities you put
  into the Holding Zone often tell you most about
  yourself. When you're ready, after you can't read-
  ily think of pure Uppers and Downers, try breaking
  down the confused ones of the Holding Zone into
  components. Example:

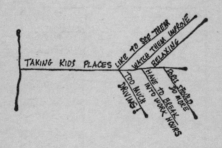

- In workshops we've held, this is where some who
  breezed through the Life pattern faltered for the
  first time. One woman said, "I guess I don't know
  what I like!" Some of us feel that we have no right

to express likes or dislikes, as if the course of our lives were determined by someone else. Quite often this reaction to making an Upper/Downer pattern has called attention to the problem: we are dissatisfied with life because we have abdicated responsibility for it.

- Make a value judgement, private and personal, on each activity. The only questions to answer are: "Did it satisfy me? Did I like it?" Try not to judge on the basis of priority, commitment, obligation, morality, or what someone else has told you should satisfy you.

Now examine all the Downers on your pattern. These may be activities that are clogging up your life's channels and preventing you from doing what you want to. Starting today, you need to eliminate, cut down on, or modify these Downers.

For each Downer, ask yourself: Do I *have* to do this? Could I eliminate it? Am I doing it for myself or someone else? How can I modify it?

It isn't enough to answer these questions in your head, because you are likely to go on living the same way, letting these Downers crowd your days and leave you feeling frazzled. You need to deal actively with each Downer. As a first pass at this, below each Downer, jot down your ideas on how to control it.

For example:

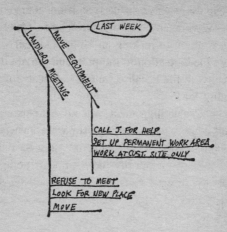

Put your Upper/Downer pattern with your Life pattern and your Wish list. You'll use it again.

Comments

- You don't have to get rid of all your Downers at once, nor could you even if you wanted to. Living well is an art, and good art has contrasts: light/ dark, high/low, up/down.

- Don't be surprised if those items you listed in the Holding Zone are your biggest time-wasters. Because they can be both enjoyable and unenjoyable, your ambivalence about them leaves you at their mercy. For example, you can watch more TV than you'd intended, enjoying it while you do, but you feel uneasy and guilty about it when you're done. Or you spend much more time with friends than you want to, and end up angry at them for wasting your time. But in either case, you don't attack the

problem, because there is a large component of
pleasure in the activity. It's part Upper, part
Downer.

- Other people have the same trouble as you in controlling Downers. For ideas on how others have
dealt with them, see Ten Time-Gobblers and How
to Starve Them.

- Rarely can you not control your Downers. For
whatever strange reasons, you may have boxed
yourself in so much that your life is more down
than up, but you made the box and you can knock
it down. How to do this is the subject of the re-
mainder of this book.

Step Three: Do It Now!

Looking back

So far you have:

1. Examined and sorted out your important roles and activities by drawing up your Life pattern.
2. Expanded your Life pattern—through your Wish list—into your areas of uneasiness: those unfinished and unstarted activities that nag at you.
3. Put a like or dislike value on the activities that fill your time (the Upper/Downer pattern).

So far you have *not*:

1. Used much time.
2. Planned, scheduled, set up time slots, or attached numbers to dreams and fantasies.

3. Done anything other than think and write words on paper.

A MODEST START, A LITTLE PAYOFF

Now it's time to *do* something. It doesn't matter much what you choose to do, as long as it satisfies you. Take out your Life pattern and your Upper/Downer pattern. What would you really enjoy doing? Chances are it's there in one of the patterns. If not, now's the time to add it.

Once again, it's up to you. You are the only one who can choose what will satisfy you.

So pick one to work on—for easy reference, we'll call it your dream. Your dream doesn't have to be a smarmy fantasy; getting the kids off to school without a hassle is as good a dream as any.

Pick a Dream

If you are harried, frazzled, fragmented, or just plain un-easy about your personal time, it's not only because you have too much to do. Hell, we all have too much to do! The reason that time weighs so very heavily on you is that you're not satisfied with most of what you do. This exer-cise provides you with a modest satisfaction: the satisfac-tion of starting to make a dream real.

So pick a dream to work on.

It might come from your wish list addenda to the life pattern, or from looking at your Upper/Downer pattern. It may be as simple as picking the first item on your wish list, or repeating an Upper. But let's not get mawkishly positive here. Never forget that some of the greatest pleasures come from the end of pain: why not snuff a Downer?

Pick a dream.

THE BASIC TOOL OF PERSONAL TIME MANAGEMENT

Now you've picked a dream to work on. It probably isn't a new one, but rather one that's been percolating for some time. How do you start realizing a dream?

If it's a modest dream—and can be done in one fell swoop—go do it! What follows is only for those dreams that can't be fulfilled in their entirety in one sweep.

Break it Down

Whatever your dream is, making it real will take several steps. It's likely that you already know these steps, but if you don't, take the time *now* to pattern them out.

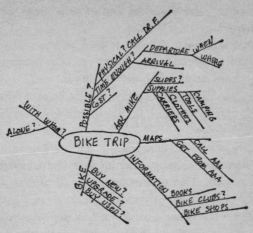

Done?

Now pick the starting steps (for example, calling to get maps, above). Remember that prying loose the first olive from the jar allows you to remove all the others, that freeing the first log loosens the whole jam, and

DO IT NOW!
READ NO FURTHER UNTIL YOU
HAVE STARTED

If You Meet Resistance

Why haven't you done it yet? Doesn't it seem odd to you that this exercise could be so hard, when all it says is, "Go do something that you want to do"?

There are standard reasons why some resist this exercise

the first time through, and there is a cheap trick that can help you past the resistance.

1. You don't really want to do what you said you did. If so, pick something else. There's certainly nothing worse than adding another Downers to your life.

2. The dream still seems too big. So break it down! The object of this exercise is to *start* something, not necessarily to *finish* it now.

3. Now isn't the time to start. Then set it up so that you can start next Tuesday, after lunch, but arrange it so you have no outs. That's a first step, as good as any.

4. Your time is really spoken for. You don't have even a free twenty minutes to take a first step. Aw, come on now! If you've boxed yourself in that much, you can unbox yourself. It's not necessary, as some people seem to feel, to go on vacation, or become violently ill, or have a heart attack in order to free some breathing time. You have to *make* time, and preferably before you're forced to take one of these drastic routes out. Helpful hint: Pick a time-consuming Downer from your Upper/Downer pattern, declare war on it for a day or a week, legislate it out of your life, snuff it! There's got to be a way to put a moratorium on something you hate doing, for just long enough to start something you like doing. Maybe the real reason is:

5. You're afraid to start. Well then, admit it and try this cheap trick:

A friend of ours who never seems to be frazzled by time scarcity, and who always seems to get everything done anyhow, has a trick he's played on himself since he was seven years old, reluctantly standing on a diving board during swimming lessons. He told himself: "I'm going to count to three, slowly. When I say 'three,' I *have* to jump. Otherwise I'll never be able to do anything again in my whole life.'' He counted and jumped. It got him off the board and into the cold water. Even today, some thirty years later, whenever he has to do something that makes him clutch up, he still runs through his ''1-2-3'' drill. It still works. And he still believes that his backbone is made of marshmallow. He still laughs when anyone mentions willpower. But he does have this cheap trick, and it works. Try it yourself.

Let's try once more:

DO IT NOW!

Step Four:
Write Your Presumé

When you were setting down your activities in the Life pattern and judging your feelings about those activities in the Upper/Downer pattern, you were examining your present and past. In a highly compressed form, you were hitting the highlights of your autobiography's latest chapters. Now you will look to the future. But we don't want you to set goals for yourself, and we don't want you to plan your life. We want you to write a *fantasy* future autobiography spanning the next six months—a *Presumé* (pronounced pray-zoo-may).

In a moment we'll tell you exactly how to start, but we want to say a few words about the name we've given it. There doesn't seem to be a word to describe it, so we've coined this one. It's a form of the personal resumé that you might write six months from now—if your fantasies all came true. Most of us have a work-oriented resumé summarizing our past work history. We could do the same for our personal lives in the past. The Presumé is such a resumé, but we write it now as if we were summarizing the next six months. The Presumé tells what we want to happen over that period.

WHAT TO PUT IN YOUR PRESUMÉ

There are three rules governing anything that goes into your Presumé.

1. It has to be something you *want* to happen.
2. It has to be *possible* (even if you don't plan for it to happen, or if it would require great energy output on your part).
3. You have to be as specific about it as possible.

For example, you feel that your life is insufferably dull. You've read a magazine article about skydiving—sounded good. Would you put skydiving into the Presumé?

1. Do you *want* to do it? If it gives you the colly-wobbles even imagining it, you may not. But if it intrigues you, put it in. Remember, it's not something you're listing as a goal; you're not *planning* to do it.

2. Is it *possible* for you? Maybe not: perhaps your coronary risk factors are high. Or you suffer from paralyzing vertigo. Or high altitudes give you a nosebleed. Or your depth perception is faulty. Then you shouldn't put skydiving into your Presumé; it's out of the question for you.

3. Suppose that skydiving has passed through the wanted/possible filter. When are you going to do it? Where? Do you want someone else to go with you? How do you find out about it? By the time you enter the skydiving fan-

tasy into your Presumé, put enough specifics into the description so that it sounds real: "In June, Mike and I went skydiving from the Livermore Airport. After the first jump I liked it so much I invited my mother to try it." An entry in your Presumé doesn't have to be as far-fetched as that one—it probably won't be (even though the example is one that actually did happen).

HOW TO START YOUR PRESUMÉ

You'll need pencil, paper, and privacy for twenty minutes. Decide what form you want to use, the one you're most comfortable with. The following examples will help you get started: Presumé of a dental technician in *paragraph* form: the *patterned* Presumé of a harried homemaker; the Presumé of an electronics engineer in *brochure* form; the fantasy *business-card* Presumé of an accountant.

> In July I realized that I was tired of being a dental technician, & that what I really wanted to do was make & sell quilts full-time. I began to save a bigger chunk of my salary until by the end of August I had enough to open my own shop. People were thrilled w/ the quality & workmanship of my quilts & soon the shop had an international reputation. "People" Magazine did a feature on me in November that quadrupled business. In December I opened a chain of quilt stores.

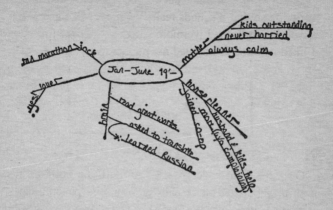

ran marathon Jack
lush lover
Jan—June 19'—
mother   kids outstanding
never harried
always calm
horse cleaner
husband & kids help
joined most (who complained)
brain
read great works
asked to translate
learned Russian

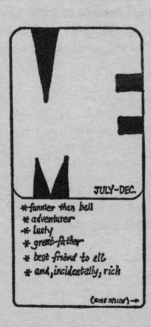

JULY—DEC.
* funnier than hell
* adventurer
* lusty
* great father
* best friend to elt
* and, incidentally, rich

(MORE INSIDE) →

```
┌─────────────────────────────────────┐
│                                      │
│         JASON REBECK                 │
│                                      │
│         well-heeled beach bum        │
│                                      │
└─────────────────────────────────────┘
```

Once the form is decided, go to it! If you need a little push to get started, look back at your Life pattern, especially the activities you added after you did your Wish list. The most favorable outcome, the most fantastic positive resolution, the most satisfying ending—these are what go into your Presumé. But you won't be able to stop there, And if you grin or even laugh while you're doing it, all the better! It's only natural to enjoy it when your fantasies are fulfilled.

Now do it.

WHAT TO DO AFTER YOU FINISH YOUR PRESUMÉ

Read it. Fold it up neatly. Stick it in the back of this book. Put a note on your calendar, for six months from today, to read it again. Forget it for awhile.

WHAT TO DO WITH YOUR PRESUMÉ SIX MONTHS FROM NOW

Read it, noting with amazement that many of the formerly unthinkable fantasies have unaccountably become real or almost real. Write another Presumé, covering the next six months.

WHAT YOUR PRESUMÉ DOES FOR YOU

Your Presumé is a list of self-fulfilling fantasies. During the six months between the time your bury it (in the back of this book) and the time you exhume it, the Presumé acts on you in a subtle and almost magical manner.

You must have had this experience: one day as you are reading, your eye fastens on a word: "threnody," for example. You don't know what it means. It bothers you, so you ask someone else or look it up in the dictionary, and in the next twenty-four hours you come across the word "threnody" at least three more times. How does that work? You may have skipped over "threnody" dozens of times before, pronouncing it "thrrrp" or "bzzzt" to yourself; it never made an impression on you. But now you have enabled conscious recognition of the word, by making the effort to learn its meaning. You have *sensitized* yourself to it.

Your Presumé operates on you in the same way. By taking the time to commit them to paper, you sensitize yourself to your fantasies. Then, over the months, you make a series of micro-choices, each of which brings you closer to realizing the fantasies. Whenever a small turning point occurs, you pivot in the direction of the fantasy, and these turning points seem to occur very often, because you are sensitized to them.

So there is no need to threnodize over your fantasies; just lay them out in your Presumé (you'll find that it's very much like hypnopaedia).

In T. H. White's classic novel about King Arthur's childhood, *The Sword in the Stone*, the most interesting character is Merlyn the magician. He can fortell the future by remembering it. Unlike the rest of us, he lives backward in time, so that what would appear to be ahead for us would be in his past. Merlyn's power of prophecy, then, depends on his memory, though he does not often call upon it consciously.

The self-fulfilling aspect of the Presumé feels much like that. By treating your fantasies as if they had already become real, by sitting down six months from now (in your imagination) and writing a review, you put yourself into the position of Merlyn the magician. When you reach a choosing point, you take the opportunity to turn toward realizing your fantasy, and it feels like a dim memory of something that has already happened—a déjà vu. You may even forget about the Presumé for half a year, but it will keep working on and for you. You can count on it.

Part Two

PAUSE

... If I had to live my life again, I would have made a rule to read some poetry and listen to some music at least once every week; for perhaps the parts of my brain now atrophied would thus have been kept active through use. The loss of these tastes is a loss of happiness, and may possibly be injurious to the intellect, and more probably to the moral character, by enfeebling the emotional part of our nature.

Darwin, Recollections

You started out with a need to do something about your conviction that you don't have enough time.

You used a little time to draw up your Life pattern, expanded it by including your Wish list, and in your Upper/Downer pattern quickly assessed how you like your present use of time, you judged how much satisfaction you get out of it.

Then you picked a dream and started to make it come true. The modest payoff in satisfaction proved to you that how you feel about what you do is more important than how much you get done.

And along the way you learned a few useful tricks like patterning.

Then you cast a magic gesture at the future with your Presumé. You put your dreams and fantasies on paper, externalizing them, then you set them aside to work on you over the next six months.

If you have faithfully done these things, check yourself over now. You should notice (1) a slight relief from the harried, breathless, hassled feeling; and (2) modest confidence that you can do what you want to.

This is a perilous juncture. Don't let your expectations grow too big yet. Before charging out where angels fear to tread, you should ask yourself what stands in your way. Unless you want to lay yourself open to more frustrations which add to your sense of not having time, answer *for yourself*:

- Can your body support your activities?
- Are your emotions and mental states getting in the way?
- Are you sufficiently irrational?

You may still feel like you'll never get it all done, but at least you've made a start on the important things. You do know better where you're heading; you know some of the activities you need to cut down on or eliminate to get there; and you've learned an important tool (patterning) and a few other tricks to keep yourself on track. You've checked your roles and activities and feelings about them. Now examine the material you have to work with: your body and mind.

Can Your Body Support Your Activities?

Your body can absorb amazing amounts of punishment, but not a steady diet of it. The plain, hard fact is you cannot go, go, go all night and all day long without bad effects on your body. You can't even lead a reasonably active life unless you tend to your body. No matter how much planning or listing or patterning you do, no matter how much you intend to accomplish, if your body isn't healthy, you won't have the energy to realize your desires.

All the muscles of the body, including the heart, deteriorate unless used. Many people scoff at this through their twenties and thirties. "I don't believe in exercise," we've all heard people sneer. "I think that putting a clown suit on and running down the street is ridiculous. I drink and I smoke and I never exercise and look at me, I'm fine." It takes little clairvoyance to foretell their future; look at their counterparts now in their forties and fifties, with their string of infirmities—bad backs, ulcers, insomnia, constipation, and the Big One, heart trouble. One senses a feeling of betrayal in them, as if the universe has let them down, and it's too late to remedy. Remember the former president, who developed phlebitis, chuckling, "When I feel the urge to exercise, I lie down until it passes." No matter what your mouth says, your body does not listen. It knows what it needs and when it doesn't get it, it protests. Certainly by now, with the Body Boom in full swing, you know that your body needs endurance or "aerobic" exercise.

"But I don't have time for exercise," you may say. Look around at active people you admire. Most of them could not accomplish what they do *without* exercise—running, walking, bicycling, swimming. They exercise because otherwise they wouldn't have the energy to do everything else they do.

When you are in shape (meaning you are not overweight, you are fairly strong, moderately flexible, and your body can process oxygen efficiently), you can count on endurance, above all. That means you can work all day and still come home ready to do whatever's on your Wish list. There are many other predictable benefits of regular exercise, too: sound sleep, an increased feeling of well-being and sexiness, regularity, relief from tension, strong attractive muscles, lowered blood pressure and heart rate, and much more. All these increase the satisfaction of being alive, too, and this is every bit as important as increased energy for getting things done as you want them.

So you must attend to your body. But how much exercise is enough for you? And what if you've tried to exercise in the past and failed to keep it up?

There is no need to despair. Start over, but start right.

First, have a thorough physical to ensure that there isn't something wrong with you—either something holding you back (like anemia) or something dangerous (like "silent" heart problems). Then be kind to yourself in the beginning. If it's taken you fifteen years to grow to your present state of flab, it's madness to think you can get in shape quickly. You'll only frustrate and possibly injure yourself by setting up an impossible exercise schedule, one that no one but an Olympic athlete could follow. Don't declare, for example, "I'm going to run a mile every day." This is unreasonable for a beginner, and after you miss the first few days, you'll probably quit. One more frustration, one more failure: exactly what you don't need.

Rather, pick three days of the week and a sport or activity that involves breathing deeply for ten to twenty minutes (such as running, walking, swimming, bicycling, or jumping rope).

Write on your calendar exactly when you will exercise. (A good time is before any meal, but it's your life, so you know when is best for you.) Then try to keep moving for at least twenty minutes each session. When you get out of breath, slow down but keep moving.

Be gentle with your body. You don't have to make exercise a grim second job. Take it slow and long and if it hurts, stop. Have faith that the exercise you've chosen, if continued regularly, will have a cumulative effect on your body. Over the coming months, you'll notice the improvement.

"But I'm too tired to exercise when I get home from work," complained one of our students. "Besides, I don't want to burn up the little energy I have left by exercising." In truth, exercise brings oxygen into your system to move that tiredness on through. Regular exercise rejuvenates you rather than tiring you out more.

And don't be discouraged if you miss exercise days. At

one time or another, everybody has trouble coaxing poor old bones out of a warm bed to exercise. Try to imagine yourself as a person who will exercise the rest of your life. If you miss a day or a week or even a month of exercise, it won't matter, because in the long run, you'll eventually ease back into the routine. Some people seem to program themselves for failure at exercise and then triumphantly give up. "I tried running every day, but the snows came and I quit." So what! Start again, but with an exercise routine that doesn't call for daily dedication. You don't have to run or swim every day, unless it feels so good that it's worth it to you.

After you've been exercising three times a week for several months, you'll be ready to step up your exercise program. Read one of the books in our reading list at the end of this section for a more accurate description of how much exercise is enough.

Your physical condition is also strongly affected by what you eat, although many choose not to acknowledge this. Most obviously and dramatically, you can be wiped out by eating too much, or by eating too little. An extraordinarily thin neighbor of ours once called, complaining of light-headedness and dizziness. She was also very depressed about her life, her marriage and her new baby.

"What have you eaten today?" we asked.

"Oh, I can't eat until tonight," she replied. "We're going out and I'm saving up for an ice cream cone and a drink."

"What does that to do with it?"

"Well, I gain weight if I eat more than 800 calories a day."

It was no feat of genius to figure out what was causing her problems. We asked her to have her doctor check her for hypoglycemia. She did much better than that: anorexia, which is a version of starvation that plagues obsessive dieters.

You eat to maintain your body. Your body's cells do not run on calories alone, they need vitamins and minerals, protein, carbohydrates, fat, and water. You cannot move, or even think, if your cells are not properly nourished. If all that your cells received in a day were shellac thinner and the chemical stew sold as ice cream, naturally you'd act a bit weird and not have the energy to do anything important for yourself.

Likewise, medicine, food additives, alcohol, and drugs all affect you, often pleasantly in the short run, but with unpleasant consequences in the long run. We're not advocating a return to roots and berries or the pure ascetic life, but you might ask yourself if some of the harriedness you experience as time scarcity might not be connected with what you put in your mouth. You could start by remembering how rushed and twitchy you felt the last time you drank too much coffee.

We have other physical needs besides such body maintenance requirements as proper nutrition and sufficient exercise. For one, body contact. Study after study has shown that babies deprived of body contact but provided with all other vital needs will die. As we grow older, we get less and less body contact from our parents, and though we learn to survive with less, it continues to affect us. As adults, we need it too, or we shrivel, not physically like the unfortunate babies, but emotionally. Look around you, at the most hurried, time-obsessed people you know. Can you imagine them hugging someone affectionately?

You can no doubt add to this brief list of physical states which interfere with getting on with a more satisfying life.

But one fact is clear: if your body needs attention, you should give it. Otherwise you may find that you can neither generate the energy to get things done nor enjoy them when you do them.

Are Your Emotions and Mental States Getting in the Way?

Your perception of time is also affected by your emotional state. If you engage in a pleasant activity in a relaxed way, time stretches, if you're aware of it at all. (How many times have you heard someone way, "Time sure does fly when you're having fun"?) But if you approach the same activity when you're agitated and tense, you are aware of the seconds clicking by and it is unlikely you will enjoy yourself.

Remember tests and quizzes at school? If you were confident and secure, you breezed through the questions; if you were nervous, you may have forgotten all you learned.

All emotional states are mirrored in your physical state and can be described in a physiological way. Anger, for example, is as much a matter of certain muscles tightening, certain hormones pouring into the bloodstream, and more shallow breathing, as it is an emotional reaction. Anger cannot be willfully banished from your system by mentally ordering it gone, without also dealing with its physical side. Those tense muscles must be relaxed; hormones must be moved on through; and shallow breathing must revert to deep breathing before anger is really gone.

Likewise, negative mental states like worry and guilt must be dealt with on all levels, including the physical, so that they do not interfere with your pleasure in living. The current American tranquilizer binge began with a recognition of these unpleasant states. But you cannot sweep negative emotions under the rug and hope they'll go away. They continue to fester and ooze out in twisted ways, one of which is definitely a feeling of never having enough time.

Deal with these emotions directly and you'll soon find that you aren't as worried about not having enough time. That sounds simple, but exactly *how* can you deal with these powerful emotions?

Again and again, we must say that you are unique. You must find your own path. What works well for others may only work partially for you or not at all. Or you might have to wage a multi-front attack on your self-defeating emotions, while your mate needs only to run or to tear paper to regain a mental balance. There are many different ways of coping.

One of the easiest and fastest ways for many to deal with worry, anger, and stress is to exercise. For example, it's been documented that after about twenty minutes of steady running, the blood level or norepinephrine, the "happiness hormone," increases. We've often felt the anger from *before* a run melt *during* a run and disappear *after* a run. (But you have to pay your dues—i.e., get in shape—first in order to be able to run twenty minutes at a time. That doesn't happen overnight.)

There are less energetic remedies for stress. Alexander Lowen, M.D., states in *Pleasure; A Creative Approach to Life* (see Reading List at the end of this section) that "in situations of stress the average person tends to hold his breath." Mentally ordering your stress to dissolve will not automatically make you breathe normally again, whereas breathing deeply may allow you to confront and overcome stress.

So does meditation, which for many people has been a way to slow down, breathe deeply, relax tense muscles, and soothe the time-troubled mind. See 9. "Waiting" in Part Three: A Bag of Tricks, for another simple relaxation process.

Others turn on when they're angry or depressed, or drink or take tranquilizers to alter their mental states. This may help if only done occasionally, but we all know someone who chronically used these crutches. The side-effects are worse than the original problem, and the problem is still there when the drug or drink wears off. As someone once said, it's like calling the fire department when your house burns, only to have them come out, turn off the alarm, and leave.

Another way to confront the emotions that destroy a comfortable sense of time is to write them down in a journal or talk to a friend or therapist. Try to break the loop of confusing emotions that prevents you from enjoying every minute of the day. Externalize through writing or talking what is haunting you internally.

After several months of keeping a journal—and it doesn't have to be done daily or even very often, just when you're disturbed—you may notice how you repeat certain behavior patterns, how you set yourself up so that you cannot take full advantage of your time or your life. This is a fruitful start at remedying the situation.

See the books in the Reading List at the end of this section if you wise to pursue these ideas for dealing with the emotions that interfere with your pleasurable use of time.

Are You Sufficiently Irrational?

Many of those who suffer most from a sense of time scarcity are admirable people. A large proportion of them pride themselves on their logical approach to life. They worship rationality for good reason: it helps them to get some things done, and they are rewarded—usually in their work—for applying it. Ironically, because they do not value their non-rational side and do not satisfy its needs, they eventually find satisfaction escaping them.

Such a person may claim that he uses time efficiently, and in a twisted way, that statement is true. He might even have a schedule covering every minute of the day, and he may attach all aspects of his life using what he calls "the scientific way," "an engineering approach," or "logic." He attempts to categorize everything in this very illogical, complicated world. All this stiff lacks, in fact, is some *life* in his life.

He becomes a victim, chained to our linear, segmented,

control-obsessed American time view (see Part Four: Perspectives for a detailed discussion of this). His efficient exertions become an end in themselves, completely dissociated from their original purpose, which was to provide a satisfying life. He jogs with a stopwatch. It has hundredth-of-a-second splits. He looks at it every other step. The man we've described is a mess, no doubt about it. But all of us share his problem, to some extent.

What exactly are we missing, or at least, not giving its proper due?

In recent years, it has been described as the "left brain/right brain split." One half of the brain, it is claimed, governs rational, logical, and verbal functions, while the other controls the pattern-recognizing, intuitive, and creative functions. One half of us is a scientist; the other, an inarticulate artist. Whether this is a metaphor or a true physiological description doesn't matter: we recognize that each of us has these capabilities.

In particular, you have a creative part of your personality (which has nothing to do with high and lofty art). If you do not cultivate this part of yourself, it withers—but you still carry its dead weight with you, in the form of feelings of desperation and frustration. Then you may wonder what all the rushing around, all the endless deadlines and hurried activity is *for*, because whatever you're doing doesn't satisfy you.

But this side of you—the creative, pattern-finding half—never really dies, regardless of how much neglect you give it. And here's the evidence: you can be feeling harried and fractured, as if there weren't enough hours in the day, and suddenly, magically, something will suspend time for you, erase those negative feelings, and heal wounds.

Here is a checklist of some healers that jog and tickle

that part of you which has no use whatever for rationality:

- *Laughter* can be so powerful that you actually cry as you laugh, and later you feel wrung out and pleasantly exhausted, as if you've been through a deep emotional experience. It can be as effective in relieving tension as crying—and men can do it, too.

  But what delights or convulses one person bores another, and any attempt to explain why something's funny to you is unfunny. Everyone thinks that everyone else has a weird sense of humor, but the oldest folk wisdom agrees with the most modern psychological thinking on this: a person who *cannot* laugh is a deeply disturbed person. When you catch yourself in a hurried, unsatisfying, humorless state, consider it a warning.

  But never forget the healing action of laughter: it can also bring you out of a harried and frustrated mood. Seek it out.

- *Sleeping/dreaming*. Some people act as though the only part of life that counts is what happens when we're awake. If these same people are "time experts," they advise you to shave an hour or two off your "sleep schedule" (a strange term!) because over a lifetime, this will "add two years to your usable time." Except for the rare occasions when cutting back your sleep is necessary, this is foolish and dangerous advice, since many important physical and emotional functions occur while you're asleep. Your muscles rest, your heart rate slows, the cells of your body repair and replenish themselves. And sleep is a quiet time in which your brain dredges up and integrates for you all the fears, hopes, and buried images that make you the unique person you are. Sigmund Freud wasn't whistling "Dixie" when he used dreams as an approach to understanding psychological problems.

Cherish those images as if they were your children; encourage them, coax them, learn from them. No matter what happens to your exterior life, no matter how dismal it may seem to you at times, you still have a rich inner life, and this is revealed to you in your dreams.

Although it is not necessary, because the activity of dreaming alone is enough, you may find additional pleasure in recording some of your dreams, either by writing or drawing. Keep a notebook beside your bed and when you have a vivid memory of a dream, either jot it down or sketch the images you saw. You will be amazed and delighted rereading over the years the dreams you otherwise would have forgotten.

Keep your dreams to yourself. They are important to you alone but usually exasperating if told in detail to others. You, too, could become the speaker here: "Hey, listen to this great dream I had last night. I was at an ice skating rink and then it was suddenly Madison Square Garden and I was an elephant only then became a snake—wait! Don't go away."

Nightmares are a form of dreaming that deserve as much attention as pleasant dreams. See the

Reading List for good information of dealing with them.

- *The arts* including handcrafts, dance, theater, and music). You also have a need to participate and observe, to make use of and enjoy all your senses. And man has worked with his hands since he became human. Today, however, we've chopped up life so much that some people claim, "I can't do a thing with my hands, can't even draw a straight line, music leaves me cold, and I don't have a creative bone in my body." This may be true, but it's also henpiddle. We believe that those people, because of a variety of unpleasant experiences (usually involving "education"), do not *choose* to include arts, crafts, and the joyful use of their senses in their lives; but we do not believe they can't do it.

You *can* learn to enjoy music; you *can* recapture the pleasure of looking at things; you *can* remind yourself that food tastes good; and you *can* start enjoying the smells of your environment. You *can* draw; you *can* sew; you *can* build. These are not talents innate to some and missing in others. It's just that as adults we are embarrassed by the ineptness of our first clumsy attempts; for some the judgment of our handwork is so painful that we'd rather not try at all. As for the pleasures of our senses, we allow ourselves to get out of the habit of noticing.

Imagine what would happen to a child who gave up trying to walk after the first failed attempt: 80 years old, in a business suit with cigar, still crawling: "No, I'm not a walker. Can't walk for beans."

You have the same innate need to create that primitive man did, whether or not what you create looks beautiful is a matter of practice and self-education. This is not to say that you could be a Leonardo de Vinci if you merely practiced enough. That level of vision is a gift. But you can bring yourself much pleasure by learning to use your hands.

Something magical happens when you use your hands to create: time seems to slow down; your mind is free to daydream, to ruminate, to coast.

The deep satisfaction this brings can erase or modify that frazzled feeling of not-enough-time, and that is why it's worth your while to learn a craft (or maybe take up gardening).

If you have never worked with your hands, you will have no idea what's possible and where to start. The classic handicrafts have arisen from the traditional natural materials—clay, fiber, wood, metal, glass, leather, dyes and pigments. The only way to find out which material you like working with best is to experiment. If you are the kind of person who learns best by being shown, take a beginners' class. If you learn best by reading, ask your public library or favorite bookstore for a well-written how-to book. And if you are really adventurous, buy a heap of clay or a pile of fabrics or a load of wood and play until the material shows you what it can do.

You are more likely to be successful in this play if you have no ultimate goal. Don't try to make a pitcher out of your clay, for example. With your inexperience, the pitcher will probably look like

Casper the Friendly Ghost and you'll end up frustrated rather than pleased. Poke the clay; cut it in half; roll it around; feel it. Make it into circles, oblongs, squares. Stack it up; knock it over; squish it down. If you need a master teacher to show you how to play, invite a five-year-old over and do everything he or she does.

You were exactly like that child, once. What happened to your capacity for play along the way?)

- In addition to your need for direct participation in arts and crafts, you can enter a magical state by observing the efforts of true artists. Color, texture, form, pattern, sound—all can affect you in pleasing ways.

  However, sometimes you have to extend yourself to reap all the benefits of art. It's almost the same as being out of physical shape; you have to realize you're reentering at a disadvantage, without the continuous years of training that make exercise pleasurable. Understanding and relishing art sometimes means doing your homework—reading about an artist, trying to understand what the artist says and why, comprehending how this particular piece of art has affected the rest of the world.

  Recently our family attended Gilbert and Sullivan's *The Mikado* for the first time. We checked a children's book our of the library to learn the story; we listened to the music ahead of time and memorized many of the songs, because they were so entertaining. The actual performance sparkled for us. We felt that we were a part of it, even seven-year-old Kali, who sang along with Koko and all the others. A few months later, we took a friend to *The Mikado*, wanting to share this enjoyment with him. Never having heard Gilbert and Sullivan before, he could not follow the spoken or sung words, and even the plot escaped him for the first half. He was bored and fell asleep. Certainly his reaction was valid for him, but with a small bit of homework, he could have enjoyed himself, instead of wasting his time.

Similarly, you can't simply put your body in a museum, say "All right, now impress me," and expect to enjoy it. You must bring something into the experience. Take along a sketch pad and pencil and try to draw some of what you see. Read up in advance, not to be knowing and impressive (as some try to do), but to expand your pleasure. And if you feel, after honestly attempting to enjoy a specific piece of art or music, that it is boring, false, pretentious, *and* a waste of time; if you have done your homework and the test fails you; then you are probably right—for you. There's a lot of crap out there. Sturgeon's lay applies here too: "Ninety percent of *everything* is crap." But the other ten percent is worth looking for, and some crap is even memorable.

If you find your time already crowded, you may have carried over from work into your personal life the practice of assigning priorities to your activities. In that case the nonrational, nonproductive, noncontrollable ones we've been examining almost certainly take low priority in your life. But these irrational activities act as a lubricant to smooth the rest of your life, and without them, your life scrapes against itself like sandpaper. The result: your time *feels* more crowded than it actually is; you rush more frantically than you need to.

Then try not to think of art, music, your senses, or working with your hands as extras. Think of them as preventative medicine. Maybe that'll raise their priority.

READING LIST

Dewey Decimal Classification numbers given in parentheses when known.

Body

Cooper, Kenneth H. *Aerobics* and *The New Aerobics*. New York: M. Evans & Co. 1968, 1970, $5.95 (613.7C).

Davis, Adelle. *Let's Eat Right To Keep Fit*. New York: Harcourt, Brace & World, Inc., 1954, $4.75 (641.1D).

Fanning, Robbie and Tony. *Keep Running*. New York: Sovereign/Simon and Schuster, 1978, $8.95.

Friedman, Meyer, and Rosenman, Ray. *Type A Behavior and Your Heart*. New York: Alfred A. Knopf, 1974, $7.95 (616.1F).

Smith, Nathan J. *Food for Sport*. Palo Alto, CA: Bull Publishing Company, 1976, $4.95.

Mind

Benson, Herbert. *The Relaxation Response*. New York: Avon Books, 1975, $1.95.

Dyer, Wayne W. *Your Erroneous Zones,* Scranton, PA: Funk & Wagnalls, 1976, $6.95 (158.1D).

Lowen, Alexander. *Pleasure; A Creative Approach to Life.* New York: Coward, McCann and Geoghegan, Inc., 1970, $5.95.

Weinberg, George H. *Self Creation.* New York: St. Martin's Press, 1978, $8.95 (158.1W).

Irrationality

Buzan, Tony. *Use Both Sides of Your Brain.* New York: E. P. Dutton, 1976, $4.95.

Koestler, Arthur. *The Act of Creation.* New York: Macmillan, 1964, $9.95 (155K).

Kohler, Mariane, and Chapelle, Jean. *101 Recipes for Sound Sleep.* New York: Walker & Co., 1965, $3.95 (616.8K).

Nicholaides, Kimon. *The Natural Way To Draw.* Boston: Houghton Mifflin, 1975, $4.95.

Part Three

A BAG OF TRICKS

Ten Time-Gobblers and How to Starve Them

Fish out your Upper/Downer pattern. When you drew it up, you put certain activities into the Holding Zone because you couldn't decide clearly whether you liked or disliked them. You probably felt ambivalent about most of them. Would it help you to know that your Holding Zone probably has the same entries you'd find in someone else's Holding Zone? Or that these activities are almost always judged ambivalently and considered as the most annoying time-wasters?

When we compiled a list of the most common gobblers of personal time, we were struck by its all-American character; it practically defines the major concerns of the average American. And the activities can all (with one exception) be described in terms of *synchronizing*.

Synchronizing is a very human activity. Toe-tapping music synchronizes your body motions with the music's beat. Soldiers and spies synchronize (through watches) before separating from their colleagues so that their actions may be simultaneous later. Even an ordinary conversation is more a dance of gestures, heavily synchronized, than a mere passage of words between two people.

The human urge to synchronize is so powerful that it even overrides strong natural rhythms. For example, it has been documented over and over that women who live together in dormitories, apartments, and kibbutzim often unconsciously synchronize their menstrual periods, probably because of subtle biochemical cues. And of course, most of us reverse-synchronize our sleeping periods with the prevailing work hours.

Our tendency to synchronize is so common that we are usually unconscious of it when it operates. We even synchronize with machines without realizing it.

You don't believe it?

The last time someone asked you if you were ready to eat lunch, did you look at your watch to see if you were hungry? And hasn't it ever struck you as funny that, with all the differences among us in physique and activity, metabolism, type and amount of breakfast we eat, we all "get hungry" at noon? Seems perfectly natural, doesn't it?

The clock is a machine we synchronize with continually, and so are the other typically American machines: the car, the phone, and the television. And these three lead the list of time-gobblers; the other gobblers on the list are similar, and the remedy for them is the same: find your best way of de-synching from them.

But first, an important question:

EXACTLY WHAT IS A WASTE OF TIME?

Say this out loud to yourself: "I am the only one who can decide when I'm wasting my time." Do it twice, for good measure, to convince yourself. It's true. No one else can tell you that what you're doing is a waste of time; during your "free" time, your home life, your personal time, *you* decide. And as we shall soon see, even in work time, it's questionable when someone else tells you you're wasting time.

Sometimes our bodies decide for us, and it doesn't matter what we've planned. You may want to finish a weekend project of trimming shrubbery, but if you need to rest because you've been working harder than your body or mind can stand, you'll find yourself resting, one way or another—watching the TV in a daze, dozing through a boring book, staring at a fire. You need to slow down, so you do. This is *not* wasting time, and in fact, ignoring these slow-down orders can be dangerous.

Even in business and industry, there are limitations to declaring what is wasted time and what isn't, and these are based on sad experience. The efficiency expert, who was a great source of popular humor in the first half of the twentieth century, isn't treated as sympathetically any more. When the Gilbreths' 1948 novel, *Cheaper by the Dozen*, poked good-hearted fun at a time-and-motion man's attempt to bring the blessings of industrial efficiency techniques to family living, it was considered hilarious. Upon rereading today, the humor seems thin and it makes you nervous.

The reality, experienced over and over, is anything but funny, and the real scenario, in business or industry, has been like this: The expert descends on the factory, watches everybody hawk-eyed for a day, and then declares so much energy is being wasted in such a way and that by following merely a few improvements, eliminating certain time-wasting motions, "efficiency" can be doubled. For a day or a week production doubles; then resentment and fatigue build up, and the accidents, fake sick leave, and even sabotage slow production to half its original output.

Victor Papanek and James Hennessey report in *How Things Don't Work* (Pantheon, 1977) that, in a nine-year period, "the automobile industry recalled 45,700,000 automobiles for inspection or repair. Many of the troubles are the result of worker dissatisfaction, and more importantly, an alienation between the worker and the product that is even more deeply rooted than the alienation between user and object . . . The dreary sameness of assembly-line procedures, the unremitting dependence by man on the timing and rhythm of the machine process, the horrifying monotony of workday and workweek are some of the primary causes of this condition."

Gearing yourself to someone else's concept of how much you can theoretically accomplish never works in the long run. You have internal rhythms and needs that you must learn to listen to and heed. Sometimes you need to be active and sometimes you need to be passive; neither one is "good" or "bad" with respect to time.

Nevertheless, you sometimes find yourself regretting the situation you are or were in. "Damn it, I wanted to finish the letter I started but that phone call came and then I was too tired and now I *still* haven't finished it and it's driving me nuts." Did you ever consider not answering the phone that night? Taking it off the hook? Telling your friend you'd call back later? Saying you'd go nuts if you didn't finish the letter, so you couldn't talk right then?

Most of the situations you call "wasting time" involve being acted upon by other people and things, synchronizing with them so that *they* set the pace. Which of the following show up on your Upper/Downer pattern? You'll get ideas for minimizing them from the following pages.

Not all of these will be bothersome to you. Perhaps, for instance, you love drop-in visits from friends and don't consider them interruptions. If so, skip the section on "drop-in visits" and move on to something that bothers you, something that *you consider a time-gobbler*.

How to use this section

This list of time-gobblers is by no means exhaustive. The human mind in its limitless creativity can turn anything into a time-gobbler. We have purposely restricted our attention to those which are responsible for 80 percent of "wasted" time.

This list, with its suggestions for removing the gobblers, is meant to *help,* and you will probably find your most bothersome time-gobbler. Jump right to it, now. Each one has suggestions for relief; each suggestion for relief has worked for someone; and for each one there is a modest first step to get you started. Go!

1. TELEPHONE

- Take the phone off the hook
- Have your calls screened
- Limit the length of incoming calls
- Remove the phone
- Remove yourself
- Let it ring
- Set up phone hours and let all your friends know

In America, the telephone is so all-pervasive that it is almost invisible and, like anything else, it can be a positive or a negative force in your life. When it saves you a 50-miles trip to a store that is closed on Saturdays, the phone is your time-saving friend. But if it rings during passionate lovemaking, it is distinctly not your friend. And when the neighborhood gossip hooks you on it, you know it can be an outrageous time-gobbler.

What is amazing is that we allow this loud machine to come between us and what we want to get done. Why, for example, wasn't the phone taken off the hook before starting to make love? Why, when having a heated discussion with friends, should we break off in mid-sentence when the phone rings? Why should you allow a phone conversation with someone you hardly like to destroy the few hours you had set aside to accomplish something on your Wish list?

Such is the power of this little machine that when one researcher randomly called the pay phones in Grand Central Station, New York City, someone always answered. "Why did you answer it?" he asked.

"Because it rang."

You are not a slave to your phone. You do not have to answer it merely because it rings. Answer it if it's *convenient* to answer it. Answer it only if you're in the mood to talk.

The phone is a tool, not a force of nature. You can use it, ignore it, and/or control it. But do take responsibility for your relationship to it. Recognize too that the telephone time-gobbler is usually a temporary one and should be treated that way. Usually you welcome word from friends via telephone; only rarely do you resent its intrusion.

Here's how others have dealt with the telephone when they don't want to be disturbed:

Take the Phone Off the Hook

Often what you want to get done requires quiet, uninterrupted time. Too often you just start, the phone rings, and even a short conversation destroys your momentum and your plans. Taking the phone off the hook solves the problem. (The busy signal is usually translated as "She's/he's on the phone. I'll call later.") Most people call back if they want to reach you, and you'll never know about the others. You will need to practice *not* explaining though:

"I've been calling you for *hours* and your line is *always* busy."

"That's right. What can I do for you?"

Usually that will take care of it. But if the caller pushes, "Why do you take the phone off the hook?" choose from this list:

"It's the only way I can get anything done."

"We didn't want to be disturbed."

"I get up at 5:30 AM, so I go to bed early."

There are a few things you'll want to be prepared for when you remove the receiver. On some phones a steady, rude blast begins minutes after the phone is off the cradle, or if anyone calls the phone company to complain. Even a stack of pillows cannot deaden this noise, so you have to try something else.

Some people (relatives, alleged friends, neighbors) are thoroughly and personally incensed that you willingly remove yourself from contact with them. If you are not absolutely clear within yourself about what it is you wish to do more than talk on the phone with them, their reaction can be very disturbing. If you find this is the case, have your calls screened.

It may be illegal to unhook your phone in some states. Check with your phone company. They will no doubt strongly disapprove of the practice, because they *want* you to talk on the phone, but usually they can't stop you.

The thought that someone such as a child or an elderly parent or Irish Sweepstakes officials might need you urgently can drive you to putting the phone back on the cradle. Such life-or-death situations are rare, and usually you will be forewarned. Under normal circumstances you can practice steely resolve by keeping the phone off the hook ten minutes at a time. The habit will grow.

Have Your Calls Screened

Here is where a business technique applies well: screening your calls. Since you don't have a secretary, others in the family or living unit can help by answering the phone for you. Ask them to say, "She can't talk right now. I'll have her call you back in half an hour." It's best to give a specific time whenever possible. This way you can group all phone calls for a time during the day or night that won't interfere with whatever you're working on. But be forewarned: If small children are helping, and they love it, be sure to rehearse them well. Otherwise, they're liable to say, "He doesn't want to talk to you," or "She's on the pot," or yell, "Hey, Dad, it's Clint! Shall I tell him you're not here?" while forgetting to put a hand over the receiver.

Others in the family or living unit hate the intrusion of the phone as much as you do, whether the call is for you or for them.Be sure you put in as much time monitoring their calls as you ask of them, and ask others to monitor for you only when necessary.

Limit the Length of Incoming Calls

Although it's difficult at first, particularly when you're caught off guard by an unwanted phone call, you can learn to limit the length of the call. If it's hard for you, practice saying out loud when you're alone and not on the phone, "I can't talk. I'm just on my way to the library," or "How good to hear from you, but I can only talk for five minutes. I'm in the middle of something." Then it's easier to say it when you need to, especially since it'll be true then.

Remove the Phone

Living without a phone is drastic and almost unheard of, but the Amish live without them, and they are known for their tranquility and longevity. Once we lived for a month with no phone and it didn't seem to interfere with our lives. We were notified of important events by mail and in person. We were offered jobs by telegram and we didn't lose any friends. For many people the appeal of hiking, backpacking, and sailing is as much nophoneness as the Great Outdoors, and we can well understand that after our month's vacation from phone calls.

A less drastic measure is to have a phone jack or cutoff installed on your phone. If it's done when the phone is installed, there's no additional fee. This means the phone rings, but you don't hear it. Call your phone company for more details.

It is not difficult to install a do-it-yourself phone bell cutoff on your own telephone, but the phone company would be distinctly unhappy if we told you how.

Some people cannot stand the thought of missing even one call. That is just the way they are, and if you suffer from this compulsion, install an answering service or device.

Some busy people go to the expense of hiring an answering service or buying an answering device that is hooked onto the phone and tapes all messages. Some devices have an override button, so that you can listen to the message-giver without their knowing you are eavesdropping. Prices range from $40 up at discount stores, with an average of over $100, and for almost everyone this is a waste of money, as well as time.

An answering device is one more machine in your life,

and rarely a time-saver. You still have to take time to listen to the tape, and good friends invariably resent talking to a machine, just as much as you do. It's a gimmick, an offensive one, and one which is rarely used for more than a few weeks, anyhow.

Remove Yourself

If you're trying to start or finish something on your Wish list and do not want to be bothered by telephone interruptions, go somewhere where you can't hear the phone—the backyard, a park, your car, the library. Of course, not all your projects and activities are portable.

Let It Ring

Whoever said you *had* to answer it? We once had breakfast with a famous prolific author, a one-hour breakfast that was carefully scheduled three months ahead to fit into the writer's busy life. At one point the phone rang and rang and the author went right on calmly eating and talking, never answering it.

The first time you choose to pass up a call, each ring seems to jangle a nerve until you want to shriek in pain. Thereafter, you learn to turn down the loudness control and ask yourself whether you want to answer the phone. Be aware, if you try this tactic, that you must have nerves of steel and a very strong desire not to be disturbed.

You might want to set up a code for close friends, like doctors do: ring once, hang up, ring twice, hang up, and then let it ring forever. You hear the code and answer (*if* you feel like talking).

Set Up Phone Hours and Let All Your Friends Know

It is not difficult to announce to friends *ahead of time*, "For the next week I'll be busy during the day. Please call after dinner only." It *is*, however, awkward to say it at the time of the unwanted interruption. Nobody intentionally bothers you; so do everybody a favor and let them know when to call. (If you can't say it directly, send out postcards.)

This method is not a panacea. Some people can't read, some don't listen; some can't remember; some don't care. This technique only works for short stretches of *specific* hard work or overwhelming desire for solitude.

2. TELEVISION

- Do something else in addition to watching
- Limit the hours you watch TV
- Study it/use it
- Don't own a TV

Everybody bitches about it; everybody sighs over it; everybody regrets watching it so much; and yet we Americans still watch hours and hours of television a day. Recently, television executives panicked when surveys showed that the average viewer had dropped to only an outrageous number of hours instead of a clearly ridiculous number of hours of viewing.

When you only have a few precious hours to yourself and when you are highly motivated to do something on your Wish list, you have no trouble shutting off the tube

ing hours of TV and may still feel too wiped out to get anything that counts (to you) done.

Don't Own a TV

Believe it or not, there are some Americans who do not own TV's. We're among that small percentage. When there's a good show on, we watch it at friends' homes—and usually end up boiling mad at ourselves. And several times we've rented a TV for a week. We've also been offered (and turned down) at least five free TVs. But we do not like the noise, the inanities, the constant hard sell, and, since we are far from steel-willed, our tendency is to watch it like zombies for hours. We'd rather spend the time enjoying each other, our child, and our lives. But this is merely a personal choice, not something we'd advise for everyone.

Other people often become instantly and aggressively defensive when they find out you don't have a TV. "But there are *great* programs on TV . . . occasionally." We generally keep our mouths shut and even feel sheepish about mentioning it here, to avoid sounding like we have a high moral purpose for not owning one. In fact, we're *afraid* of it, like we're afraid of heroin.

But in our fantasies, this is what we would preach: Suppose you hire a new babysitter. She teaches your children that the funniest thing in the world is to hit someone on the head with a banana, urges them to eat foods which you know are bad for them, tells them that they should demand that you buy them expensive toys, and teaches them tricks to make you buy them. The role model she offers your kids is psychotic: she shows them that it's better to be stupid, that it's more important to be popular than anything else, and that anyone who buys the right products can be both stupid and popular. And she tells them that they should sit still watching her for four or more hours a day while scarfing down those bad foods . . . Would she last long in your house? This is a personality profile of the most popular babysitter in America—your television set.

3. CAR TRIPS

- For commuting, use other methods
- Group errands and taxi services

Remember how eagerly you waited for your sixteenth birthday, so you could drive? You couldn't believe then that you'd ever *not* want to drive the car. But now that honeymoon is over. You no longer love spending hours behind the wheel; instead of making you feel exhilarated, driving leaves you feeling exhausted, too beat to tackle anything with pleasure.

There is a physiological reason why driving tires you. As reported in *The Western Way of Death*, every time you step on the accelerator, adrenaline shoots through your body, exactly the same way gas shoots into the car's engine. The adrenaline prepares you to fight or flee, just as it did for our ancestors when they faced saber-toothed tigers. But behind the wheel of a car, you can't really fight or flee, so you're left with a churning, chemical broth in your bloodstream and a feeling of extreme exhaustion.

It eats up your time, too, and there's not much else you can do while sitting on the freeway during rush hour, or driving around and around the block to find parking, or zigzagging from piano lessons to school to the orthodontist, or driving hard for four hours so you can spend one exhausted weekend at the beach and then drive back.

This is not meant to be a tirade against the automobile. It's a pleasant and useful machine. But if yours tires you and you resent some or all of the time spent driving it, here are suggestions to help you.

For Commuting, Use Other Methods

Use one or a combination of the following: car pools, public transportation, bicycle, moped, walking. Sometimes all it takes is a change in attitude, keeping in mind that it won't always be easy or convenient to break the habit of driving. Merely deciding that you're not going to drive that car all the time opens up approaches you may have ignored before.

We know a man who takes a city bus to the train, rides 30 miles to his work city, and walks the last mile to work. He finishes reading a novel every other day on the train and feels great from walking.

Senator William Proxmire, in his sixties, is known for running five miles to work and home every day.

A local engineer rides his bike 15 miles to work and home every day, rain or shine. He beats his car-driving neighbor home through rush-hour traffic by ten to fifteen minutes.

Keep in mind that you don't have to overturn totally your car habits (which probably wouldn't work anyway). You can test a new way to commute, ease into it. At first, why not stop driving just one day of the week? Park your car a half-mile or mile from work and walk or bike or start riding your bike on weekends, so you can slowly build up to whatever mileage is needed.

Remember that this is an automobile country. It is not easy to find alternatives to the car. On the other hand, you can easily find a thousand reasons for you you can't leave your car at home: "It takes too much time to bicycle"; "I get too sweaty walking"; "There's no public transportation."

But nobody out there is making you drive that car, so why are you arguing? It's you against you. Does commuting by car tire you, prevent you from doing what counts in life? Then with some effort, you can find alternatives to driving. Ask around at work to find out how other people get there. Ask your friends for ideas to help you solve your unique transportation problems. Ask your city, county, state transportation departments what they recommend.

Group Errands and Taxi Services

Try to group errands and taxi services so that you can accomplish them in one outing. It is more exhausting and expensive to make three short trips than one long one. When you are headed for the car, ask yourself, "Do I really have to do this *now?* Could I put it off until later?"

As for taxiing children around, the single loudest complaint of suburban mothers, this is something you've brought on yourself, by your choice of where to live and your personal priorities. If you are trying to raise children who are independent, have a common-sense knowledge of themselves and their capabilties, and have the energy to pursue their own interests, are you really doing them any favors by driving them everywhere? They grow up waiting for someone else to make their decisions, make the arrangements to implement their decisions, and then figuratively, wait for someone else to drive them to the action. Those "adults" are not ready for mature living.

One woman we know was greatly perturbed by her new so-called idyllic life in the country. "In the morning I would pack a thermos of coffee, a lunch, and a stack of magazines and books in the car. Then I drove my four teenagers down the hill to school and spent the whole day in the car, driving them to the dentist, the music lessons, swim team, gymnastics, and then sat waiting for the next trip. I was a basket case every night. Finally, we decided that we think it's more important for the kids to get themselves around and for me to do something for myself, so we sold the house in the country and moved right back to the city. Now the kids ride bicycles everywhere and I've gone back to work. Everybody's happier."

Some people's images are so tied up in being "good" mommies and daddies, doing right by the kids, sacrificing everything so the children will have sports and music and dancing and art in their lives, that saying "No, I won't drive you" to a kid is threatening. These same people often go through difficult times in their forties and fifties when the kids no longer need them. The foundation of their self-image, built on kids, is ripped away and they flounder. Supermom, meet Valium. Valium, meet Supermom.

4. TRIVIA

- Advertising
- Idiot work
- Habits
- Gadgets

What you consider trivial or unimportant, such as doing the Sunday crossword puzzle, someone else may consider important to the enjoyment of Sunday. Only *you* can define your own trivia. But if you do not recognize your trivia when you step in it, great amounts of your precious free time disappear, leaving you with a bewildered feeling: "My god, what happened to the time? I know I was here and I know I was doing *something*, but what have I got to show for it?"

No one else is going to swoop down out of the sky and control your trivia for you. We're all struggling with our own dose of it, so you're the only one who can choose to shut off or limit how much the trivia in your life nibbles away at your free time. One way to identify your own trivia is to examine your Upper/Downer pattern. Everything below the line probably has a high trivia component and the items in the Holding Zone probably do, too. But it may be helpful to you to see how others handle these four classic categories of trivia.

Advertising

Modern advertising has developed into such a science of hypnosis that you can consider yourself effectively hypnotized whenever you open a magazine or newspaper or turn on the TV. Those wizards, the advertisers, can't make you stick pins into your thigh or sing silly songs like a stage hypnotist can, but they can put you into such a trance that you read articles and watch shows that aren't even interesting to you. They know how to keep your attention so you'll stick around when the commercial comes on. Their object is to sell you their product, but you lose a lot of time while they have you glued to the set.

If you feel there is a lot you are not getting done and yet you still watch shows that aren't particularly interesting and continue to read articles and books in spite of a lack of interest, you will have to make a choice: either drown in this trivia or control the trivia.

Some people are of such an addictive nature, ourselves included, that we can only control trivia by banishing it, shutting it off completely. Whenever we have had a TV in our house, we've watched it non-stop, dumb programs, dumb commercials, and all. We hardly spoke to each other for days because we were staring straight ahead at the magician's box. (As for our love life, oy!) Perhaps you can turn it off at will. We can't. Since we're reluctant to watch it long enough to form calluses and it interferes with living, we don't have a TV at all.

We also apply the Rule of One to books and articles: if the author doesn't interest us in the first paragraph of the first page, we are tempted to close the pages. There are so many wonderful books and magazines that pass this test, why waste time reading what we don't enjoy? As for slow-building, well-crafted writing, we require strong word-of-mouth recommendations before we violate the Rule of One. And there are classics of literature that we haven't been able to squeeze past the Rule, no matter how many times we've tried.

Idiot Work

Any activity that is repetitive, never-ending, time-consuming, and *which you resent doing* is idiot work. Unfortunately, there is idiot work you cannot completely eliminate, such as housecleaning or maintaining your possessions, but you can minimize the irritation of doing it.

A corollary to Parkinson's Law says that idiot work tends to expand to fill all your available hours. This suggests two tactics: (1) do your creative, satisfying activities first (and conversely, never do the idiot work first), and (2) allot a reasonable but niggardly amount of time to idiot work, set a timer, and quit when the timer rings, no matter what kind of a mess you leave.

Housework

Cleaning the dwelling is a never-ending job that almost everybody resents. It is an activity charged with guilt, and not merely a matter of keeping your living areas sensibly livable. How many times have you been invited to enter the front door with, "You'll have to excuse the mess . . ."? How many times have you said it yourself? Often, the only mess visible is a magazine which is not lined up at right angles to the coffee table.

Before applying the two tactics suggested above to housework, you should attempt to scan your attitudes about it. Many of these attitudes are totally irrational. Whether you're a Compulsive Neat or a Pigpen, you probably have a picture of an Ideally Clean Home tucked away in the back of your head, one so impossibly neat and organized, so operating-room sterile, that you could never achieve that degree of perfection. And no wonder—soap, appliance, and furniture manufacturers have spent billions for advertising to give us that image of unattainable perfection. Guilt pushes product.

At the risk of being called un-American, we modestly propose that most people already keep their houses or apartments reasonably clean, sensibly organized, and moderately neat; that there is little chance that such a home will turn into a virulent pesthold in a day, a week, or even a month; that the only people who really disapprove of the "mess" of your home live in TV commercials and not down the street; and that dust-bunnies under your bed will not give you a social disease. Our suggestion: relax.

Having said that, we must admit that you still need to keep your home moderately neat, sensibly organized, and reasonably clean. The two tactics suggested above—idiot work last, and set a time limit—apply to housework, but only when you are more or less caught up on it. It is when you are perpetually behind that you drive yourself nuts. Extrication then calls for emergency measures:

1. Reserve a weekend or several days for nothing but housecleaning. Remember spring housecleaning bashes of yesteryear? There was a reason for them: our ancestors got behind, too. And like them, you should get help. Enlist your family or trade a similar weekend of work with friends, find high school help, or hire a housecleaning service. Plan to move every piece of furniture you have, clean those gritty corners, reorganize the shelves, wash all the windows, shampoo the rugs, scrub the floors, and throw away everything you can (better yet, send it to a charity organization). When you are through, you are (theoretically) caught up. Now you must look ahead so you don't get behind again.

2. Make a list of all the cleaning jobs you feel you must do each week, vacuum each room, dust, etc. Decide how often you want to clean—once a week, three times a week, a little every day—whatever you wish. Now turn to the One-Week Calendar in the Appendix and divvy up the cleaning so that all the work gets done.

Set a timer limit to each cleaning session and quit when the timer goes off. Here's a half-hour a day schedule (in addition to the nightly blitz of the house):

Sunday	Monday	Tuesday	Wednesday
garden	vacuum and dust all rooms	mop kitchen, bathroom, eating porch	sweep driveway and front steps

Thursday	Friday	Saturday
vacuum all rooms	do miscellaneous cleaning and reorganizing of piles	do outside housework

Here's the same amount of work done three times a week for one hour each time (again, set timer):

Sunday	Monday	Tuesday	Wednesday
nothing	vacuum and dust all rooms; sweep driveway and front steps	nothing	mop kitchen, bathroom, eating porch; do miscellaneous cleaning and reorganizing of piles

Thursday	Friday	Saturday
nothing	nothing	do outside housework; gardening

If you only want to clean once a week, then squeeze it all into a one-day orgy (but it usually feels better to do a little every day or every other day).

Now you know what you're *supposed* to do, whether you do it or not. And if you don't get the dusting done this Tuesday, the world won't fall apart before you do it next Tuesday. Remember, no one else knows or cares about that dust-bunny behind the dresser.

3. Make a list of your once-a-month and once-(or more)-a-year cleaning jobs like washing windows, cleaning the garage, shampooing rugs, turning the mattress, and cleaning winter coats. Divide these special jobs up over the year and write them down on the One-Year Calendar in the Appendix.

Now you can apply the two tactics that keep idiot work from destroying your pleasure: allot a time limit to it and do it *after* you do the important things in life.

We know a woman who works full-time but who is also a budding songwriter. Meanwhile she lives in a house which gets annoyingly dirty. Every night when she gets home from work, she writes songs or reads or listens to music until midnight, at which time she spends an hour cleaning house. She never allows housework to interfere with her songs because as she says, "I can clean the house when I'm tired from writing songs, but I can never write songs when I'm tired from housework."

We do all our housecleaning between 7 and 8 AM when we're also getting breakfast and our daughter ready for school (we get up at 5:30 AM to start more satisfying activities). One of us cooks and does the once-a-day dishes, the other makes the bed and starts the laundry. Then we do together whatever's on the list for that day (vacuuming, dusting). At night all three of us blitz the house before kali goes to bed, picking up and putting away.

If housecleaning particularly annoys you, you might en-
joy reading *Nobody Said You Had To Eat Off the Floor;
The Psychiatrist's Wife's Guide to Housekeeping* by Carol
G. Eisen (David McKay, 1971, $6.95).

And remember, every time you get behind, get help to
catch up—which for some, could mean weekly help. You
can find such help through the newspaper want ads, through
listings in the telephone Yellow Pages, at your local high
school or college employment office, or by asking around
for recommendations from friends. A less expensive way
is to form a house-cleaning co-op with two or three friends,
so that periodically everybody scrubs one home together.
And to put things into perspective, an extensive survey has
shown that despite all the time-and-labor saving devices
used, today's housewife spends *more* time at housework
than her grandmother did in 1924.

Maintenance

Nothing can be more depressing than having every free
minute taken by a house in constant need of repair, a lawn
that needs mowing, a car that won't start, a tool you can't
find to fix the car because the garage is an unholy mess.
What's depressing is not that this work is never-ending and
time-consuming, but that it's never what you want to be
doing at the time.

Most of it can be anticipated and a little preventive care
practiced, so that you're not always responding to emer-
gencies. Your car, for example, can be kept running
smoothly for years if you regularly clean the spark plugs,
change the oil, have four lube jobs a year, and change dirty
filters twice as often as recommended (see "How To Make
Your Car Last 20 Years" by Wade A. Hoyt in the Bibli-

ography at the end of the book). You can have a garage do this for an exorbitant fee, or you can buy the repair manual for your car, as well as a few inexpensive tools, and learn quite easily how to do it yourself. Two great books are John Muir's *How To Keep Your Volkswagen Alive* and the repair manual written for your car, available at auto supply stores or from the dealer.

Turn to the One-Year Calendar section on page 199 and schedule these maintenance sessions throughout the year, as suggested.

Other idiot work can be eliminated by rethinking your alternatives. A lawn, for example, can be an excess you don't need in this day of dwindling natural resources. You have to water it, weed it by hand or with poisons made from precious petroleum, fertilize it with the same, cut it via hand or gasoline-powered mower, and dispose of the cuttings either in the compost heap or at the dump. Do you really need a lawn? Could you get along with half lawn, half bark? Do you use your lawn? Does it use you?

Your car? Could you cut its use in half if you commuted by bicycle, walking, public transportation? Even if you only cut out driving one day a week, you'd save yourself a great deal of time, money, and anguish over a period of years.

The question is, are you a prisoner of your possessions? If so, consider eliminating some, simplifying the maintenance of others, and anticipating the care of those you choose to keep.

Habits

Most of our habits we defend jealously, and with reason—
we need small personal rituals. These habits comfort and
feed our souls, whether we acknowledge that fact or not.
But other of our habits are personally destructive and time-
gobbling. Again, only you can decide whether it is to your
advantage to break a habit or not.

An example is the person whose energy peaks in the
morning. On weekends if he doesn't start what's important to him right away in the morning, it usually does not
get done, which leaves him feeling vaguely uneasy and
dissatisfied all weekend. Unfortunately, this man loves
to start the day by reading the morning newspaper. On
weekends, since he has more time to do than than during
the week, he tends to read everything, even the shipping
columns. He's not really interested, but it's habit, and
because of it, he sometimes does not get moving until
noon, at which time he does not have the energy to start
anything on his Wish list, one of which is to repair his
boat. An early-afternoon nap finishes off the day, with
predictable grouchiness after. The varnish continues to
flake off his boat.

One Saturday he tried getting up and going right to work
on the boat and found that by his mid-morning break, during which he briefly scanned the paper, he had built up a
momentum which carried him into mid-afternoon. Now he
normally operates that way. From time to time he still falls
back into his old habit of reading the newspaper first thing
Saturday morning, but since he knows what he's doing,
it's a pleasant break from routine, rather than habitual time-
gobbling.

Sometimes your time-gobbling habits are hard to break.

Once you identify these habits, you have to decide whether you want to break them (if they stand in the way of doing whatever is important to you) or modify them. For help, read *How To Make and Break Habits* by J. Robbins and D. Fisher (Peter H. Wyden, Inc., 1973, $5.95) or *Science and Human Behavior* by B. F. Skinner (Macmillan, 1953, $6.95).

Gadgets

Keep in mind that study after study shows that the more gadgets and machines with which you complicate your life, the less time you have to enjoy that life. If you feel harried a good amount of the time, consider cutting down the number of gadgets you own.

During your spring cleaning take everything out of the cupboards, shelves, garage, and attic and ask yourself how crucial each item is to your life. Do you really use the electric potato peeler every day? If you have to put 25¢ in a machine in order to use it, would it be worth the money? If you can't bring yourself to have a giant garage sale and sell off everything non-essential, then pack it away in the garage for awhile and see if you miss it at all.

Suppose that a gadget is useful, though. Do you waste time using it just because you own it? Most gift gadgets are like that, as well as most "ecologically sound" modern conveniences, like trash compactors. Heave things like this whenever you can, or better yet, never let them get into your home.

Each gadget you get rid of gives you that much more free time to do what you really want to do.

5. SHOPPING

- Shop at quiet times
- Be informed before you buy
- Anticipate your purchases
- Group your errands
- Buy in bulk
- Shop by mail

Nothing is as energy-sapping and time-wasting as having to shop for groceries at 5:30 PM in an adrenaline-charged, crowded supermarket because there's nothing to eat at home. Not only do you spend more time waiting in line than shopping, but also the unpleasantness lasts the rest of the night.

For many people shopping for anything is the biggest time-gobbler of all. But since we have to eat, cover our bodies, and please our friends and family, we might as well learn to deal with shopping intelligently. Here's how others handle it.

Shop At Quiet Times

Most people already try to shop this way, but if you don't make it a habit. Call the store manager or scout out the slow hours at the supermarket and arrange to shop during them.

Be Informed Before You Buy

How exasperating it is to spend $300 for a ten-speed bike that won't shift when you bring it home. By reading *Consumer Reports,* you might have learned that the price of that particular brand is higher than its quality because of a massive, costly advertising campaign, whereas a lesser-advertised but cheaper bike is actually a better buy. Instead of making one "time-consuming" half-hour trip to the library before buying, you've just spent $300 for a piece of junk that you take back to the bike shop three times, one hour each trip, fiddle with each time you bicycle, and eventually sell in disgust.

Uninformed buying is the ultimate time and money-waster. To cut down on it, plan to research in the public library before every major purchase you make. Be wary of magazine equipment surveys, though, if the magazine carries advertising. Too often the magazine will never tell the whole truth about an advertiser's product. Magazines like *Consumer Reports* help you make wise money decisions.

When you make minor purchases, do whatever you can to avoid impulse buying. It won't be easy, because the object of most marketing is to lure you into buying on impulse. The consumer movement (which at the time of writing seems to be losing momentum) has performed the valuable service of reminding us that buyer and seller are adversaties—something our grandparents took for granted. Remember that, the next time you really *want* to buy something you don't need. The sellers pump up the impulses. Stores wisely put a time limit on sales to pressure you into buying while the impulse is strong. The best defense against impulse buying is:

IF YOU REALLY WANT IT, WAIT A MONTH BEFORE BUYING!

No impulse lasts that long. And if that irresistibly desirable object won't be on sale a month from now, why you can save even more than by not buying it at all.

Also ask as many experienced people (*not* the sales-men!) as you can about the reliability of various brands. When we were about to leave on a cross-country bicycle trip, our best information sources were experienced cyclists, who warned us about certain brakes that don't stop you on mountains, equipment racks that break off, and seats that split, leaving you sitting on a 2-inch seat-post.

Anticipate Your Purchases

Sales

There is a standard cycle of sales for necessary items. We've put it with the One-Year Calendar in the Appendix. If you can ease your way into shopping for next year's bathing suits in July, buying clothing in January, and Christmas cards on December 26, you can save a great deal of last-minute running around, as well as a great deal of money.

Gifts

Gifts do not have to be the pain they often are if you anticipate them in two ways: (1) write in the person's birthday or anniversary or the celebration on the One-Year Calendar. Then write it again two to four weeks *before* the date, to remind yourself to buy, make, or wrap the present or to send the card; and (2) buy presents and cards whenever you see something the person would like, stockpiling these throughout the year in one special off-limits drawer, box, suitcase, or shelf. No more last-minute scrambling for gifts. (Be *sure* to label what's in it and who it's for if you prewrap these gifts; otherwise, you'll give the razor to the second-grader and the Silly Putty to Uncle Ed.)

If you prefer to make all your gifts, start early, like in July for Christmas gifts. For each of the last few years, we have chosen a general theme for presents; everybody receives a variation of it. One year it was bags and totes (backpacks, needlework cases, purses, camera bags); the next year it was silk-screening (T-shirts, calendars, prints). This makes the selection for each person easier.

Some unusual gifts we've heard about are: a promise to a wife from a husband to do all the cooking and cleaning for an entire month; an outing in a hot-air balloon; a tree planted in the person's name in a park; the delivery in bed of *The Sunday New York Times* with coffee, bagels, cream cheese, and lox. Not one of these gifts required bucking crowds.

If you resent the yearly dash for gifts, you might think about the meaning of gifts and the slavery they can impose on your life. Read *The Meaning of Gifts* by Paul Tournier (Pillar Books, 1976,) $1.25) and consider not giving gifts at the dictated times at all. We grew to resent Christmas materialism so much that we now gift our loved ones on *our* birthdays, preferring to give willingly at our own choosing rather than resentfully at someone else's.

Group Your Errands

Most shopping, and in fact, almost any errand, is *not* urgent. Here's a trick that helps you keep errands in proper perspective. Keep pads of paper (see Tools of Organization in the Appendix) in every room you live in and also one central errand box or envelope. Your brown shoes need repairing? Write it down and throw it in the errand envelope. Then once a week (or as seldom as possible, if you really hate errands) take out all the notes and arrange them geographically, so that when you go to the bank, for example, you also pick up the color slides, leave the coats at the cleaner, buy sunglasses at the pharmacy, and drop off the brown shoes. If any errands call for a single trip, throw the slip back into the errand envelope and wait until you can group three or four more around it before going. You'll be amazed how, with a little practice, you can make any errand nonurgent. Don't do errands in your prime creative time. Treat them as idiot work.

Buy In Bulk

Bulk buying saves you money and time. We're talking about more than buying rice by the pound instead of by the ounce. Develop an attitude, not a list of products you buy a lot of: buy a roll of first-class stamps, rather than a few at a time; take the time to select comfortable sensible shoes and then buy two pairs.

Running shoes, for example, cost about $30 a pair at this writing. To pay $60 for two pairs may temporarily bankrupt you, but (1) you won't have to take the time to buy another in two years; (2) by alternating shoes, both will last longer than one pair worn day after day; and (3) a year from now, at the current rate of inflation, one pair will probably cost $60.

Shop By Mail

When this country was more rural than urban, people spent winter months pouring over mail-order seed and merchandise catalogs (like Sears, Roebuck and Co. and

Montgomery Ward). Then when we all moved into the cities, we began to visit neighborhood stores, where we could feel the fabric and try it on for fit before buying. But today, too often a time-consuming, exhausting visit to the stores yields nothing. Clothes, for example, are poorly made, don't fit, and cost a fortune, so you go home empty-handed.

Maybe it's time to go back to shopping by mail, and not only for clothes. With some searching, you could probably find a mail-order catalog for any product you need. We've even heard of weekly groceries ordered by mail.

Some mail-order guides worth seeing are: *The Catalogue of American Catalogues; How To Buy Pratically Everything by Mail in America,* Maria Elena de la Iglesia, Random House, 1973, $4.95; *The New Catalogue of Catalogues; The Complete Guide to World-Wide Shopping by Mail,* Maria Elena de la Iglesia, Random House, 1975, $7.95; *The Goodfellow Catalog of Wonderful Things/Traditional and Contemporary Crafts,* Christopher Weills, Berkley Windhover, 1977, $7.95; and *The Last Whole Earth Catalog,* Stewart Brand, Portola Institute/Random House, 1971, $5.00.

6. CLUTTER, MENTAL AND PHYSICAL

- Identify and organize
- Write it down
- Simplify, eliminate, live with it

Active people generate active messes. If we are to live full, active lives, it is unlikely that we will exist in a state of no-mess. Clutter is not so much a matter of having too many things floating around, as not knowing where to put all those loose things. It's a variable nuisance. One day you'll be driven to distraction by the mess of unsorted papers and bills on your desk. You decide you can't get anything done unless you tackle that mess first. Another day, knowing that it would only take five minutes to master the mess because you've set up an organizing system for it, you ignore it until you've done something important first. Same mess, but one day it's maddening and the next, it's nothing.

This applies to mental clutter too. When there are too many irritating dates and appointments and phone numbers and ideas and obligations skittering around in our heads, it interferes with our enjoyment of life right now. We dash around, trying to keep track of everything and end up frazzled and harried. The accepted description is "a chicken with its head cut off."

Everyone has a different tolerance for clutter, but generally the older you are, the more an unorganized mess bothers you. Here's how others cope with it:

Identify and Organize

For some perverse reason the authors both have a tendency to pile things in doorways and pathways, and on our work surfaces—books, junk, laundry baskets, papers. Then we spend a ridiculous amount of time maneuvering around the piles as if they were land mines. The time spent dodging clutter is, objectively, small; the annoyance we feel magnifies it subjectively.

The path to the laundry room at the back of the garage, for example, which we visit at least every other day, was

for too long a zigzag around sawhorses, boxes of unsorted
tools, bikes, a pile of lumber, and the camping equipment.
Every time we did the laundry, we swore all the way
through the obstacle course and all the way back. This was
insane.

Attack such a clutter by sorting:

1. What in this mess do I use every day? Put these in
one pile.

2. What do I use occasionally? Put these in a second
pile.

3. What have I not used for years, and what do I not
use here? Put these in a third pile.

Now look at the first every-day-use pile and ask yourself, where do these belong so that they are close to the
work area where I use them? Put them there. Put the oc-
casional-use items in the surrounding drawers, shelves, and
cupboards. Put the never-used pile in a box and move it
away from the clutter area. For the most part, these items
can be given away or sold. (But if you have space to store
them and label them clearly, you'll be able to find them
again).

Since your living patterns are constantly changing, be
prepared to reassess constantly. To keep yourself from pil-
ing new messes in your pathway, sort as soon as you notice
one forming. You can sort a half-dozen little clusters faster
than one enormous one.

All of this is fine if you have the proper storage space.
But you might have to use your available space cleverly.
In a cupboard, for example, all the plates, glasses, and
cups may be squished together on a shelf, while there is 8
inches of dead space above, between them and the next
shelf. By screwing cup hooks into the underside of the

shelf above to hand the cups on, space is freed on the shelf for something else you use every day.

But we have yet to find anyone who feels he or she has enough storage space at home. For more ideas on simple, inexpensive storage systems, see Tools of Organization on page 207.

Write It Down

Buy a calendar that has enough space to write all appointments and reminders. Think carefully how you will use the calendar, so you don't waste time (and money) on a useless one. We were given a beautiful one-year calendar with one-inch squares for each day. After struggling for a few weeks to squeeze our handwriting into those tiny squares, we decided that we would look at the beautiful prints, but buy a calendar we could write on comfortably. You don't *have* to use what you're given if it's inconvenient to your living pattern.

Will you carry the calendar around? Should it fit in a pocket? Do you like to see the week at a glance or the whole month at a glance? Will others in the family write in it too? Should it be hung next to the phone?

We use our calendar to write down the usual doctors' appointment, birthdays (we also write a reminder to ourselves two weeks ahead), special events, reminders ("call so-and-so"), school holidays, yearly maintenance reminders (cars, teeth, rugs), taxes, and all other mental clutter that does not need to muck up our brains.

We also stash 5 × 3″ notebooks with pens in every coat pocket to write down great ideas, reminders of what we've forgotten, sketches, snatches of conversation,

books we want to read, and so forth. Many of these pages
have to be ripped out and transferred to the calendar and
files at home later, which is not totally efficient but works
best for us. Some people prefer to carry 3 × 5″ index
cards around with them, for easy filing later.Stick with
whatever works best for you. We know a dermatologist
who carries around a tiny pad of pregummed labels in
her pockets. On these she jots reminders, dates, appointments. Then she sticks these on her calendars, at home
or at work.

Keep pads of scratch paper with pens (attached by
string if you don't want them to disappear) in every room,
especially near the phone, refrigerator, toilet, bathtub,
bed, and table. The ideas and reminders that bob to the
surface of your brain ignore clocks and have scant regard
for what you're doing. Capture them as they occur by
writing them down, and you'll free your mind from unnecessary clutter.

Simplify, Eliminate, Live With It

Sometimes it's best to ignore clutter. Once Robbie was
under a nonstretchable deadline. She had always felt she
couldn't start work in the morning until the dishes were
done and the bed was made, both of which broke up her
stretch of most creative time and often left her stalled in
mid-morning. So in order to finish the book, she asked
Tony to take responsibility for the bed and dishes. "Sure,"
he said, grinning, "I'll take charge."

For the next six weeks Robbie never gave it another
thought. Neither did Tony. The bed was never made, but
the world went on, the book got written, and the hydran-

geas bloomed. Under the conditions, making the bed was a time-waster that was temporarily eliminated. The dishes were washed when needed, too, and weren't a drag on creative time.

If you have duties that you resent, like the Downers in your Upper/Downer list, ask yourself, "Would life go on if I didn't do this now?" If you have clutter in your home or mind, could you temporarily ignore it so it doesn't gobble up your free time?

7. DROP-IN VISITS

- Confront them head-on
- Schedule times together
- Enjoy your friends

The first time your old college friends who just moved to town drop in unannounced before dinner, you're delighted. The second time they come over unexpectedly just as you're planning your spring garden, you feel mildly irritated. The third time they show up, you either grit your teeth and act unfriendly all night despite yourself, or you face it and express this message as politely as you can: "Please call before you come over." Remember, they are never going to know what bothers you unless you communicate it to them, but they will sense that something's not right between you.

It's not a good idea to be so unfriendly that no one cares to come see you. We need our friends to enrich our lives, just as we need art and dreams and laughter and exercise;

and in order to have friends, you must spend time together, exchanging ideas, doing things together.

At any rate, it isn't the friends you object to, it's the interruption. So you need your friends, but you still need time for yourself. How else are you going to get it all done? Here's how other people solve the problem of drop-in visits:

Confront Them Head-On

At the time that a friend of ours first became interested in photography, she had only the few hours to herself in the afternoon when the baby slept. When someone came to the door, she learned to say, "I'm sorry, but I can't let you in; this is my darkroom time. I'll call you at dinner time."

Even more direct is to say, "In the future, could you call before you come over?" But who can say it easily the first time? Although it may feel awkward momentarily, nobody gets so incensed that they drop you as friends, and hardly anyone ever takes it badly. On the contrary, friends usually value and respect that kind of honesty. It also helps if you add, "That way I'll enjoy your company more." (But then again it may not.)

Sometimes what you had planned to do when you were interrupted can't easily passed off to others as high-priority. A mother suddenly finds herself with the prospect of two pure hours of quiet before the kids come home. She brews a cup of tea, picks up a great trashy novel, and heads for a long, soaking, totally frivolous bath—when the doorbell rings. The neighborhood mouth arrives and doesn't leave until the kids come home. The mother can't bring herself to say, "You can't come in because I'm going to take a bath."

Learn to say "Hell, come in, but I can only give you 15 minutes." You do not have to explain or apologize at all—it's *your* life.Then set the timer for 15 minutes and put it where you can hear it ring, but not tick. Get out of the chair and move to the door after it rings.

You can be firm without being rude, assertive without offending. But you will have to make the first move; nobody else will do it for you. After all, it's not a sin to run your own life instead of, by default, letting others run it for you.

Schedule Times Together

Take the initiative and schedule visits.A woman executive who now travels widely and works long hours used to be a housewife, with her daytime hours "free." The friends she had then became miffed about not seeing her once she started working, so she made a list of her friends. Now she routinely set up one lunch every week with the next friend down the list. She realizes they'd be furious if they knew how methodically she goes about it. "But my days are full and weeks could easily slop by without seeing anyone. Then they'd really be mad. These friends mean a lot to me, but so does my work, so I actively schedule time for my friends."

Some people have cocktail parties; some have dinners; some purchase season tickets with (and for) friends to theater or sports events; some have parties at night; some have fitness sessions together and exercise while they catch up on news. Since we're early risers and nondrinking jocks, late-night bashes do not appeal to us. We like to have our friends over for Sunday morning brunch with a walk afterward.

Remember that no matter how carefully you schedule, some people will still drop in. If you care—and sometimes you're delighted with the interruption—you'll have to deal with it directly.

Enjoy Your Friends

Who says that every visit is an interruption, or that every interruption is bad? A welcome friend doesn't interrupt, by definition.

Taking responsibility for your choices helps here. If you *choose* to spend time with a friend, you have no call to complain about not getting something else done. Consider it a better-than-even trade-off.

8. MEETINGS

- Use patterning
- Attend for a limited length of time
- Don't go
- Keep your hands busy

Without a strong, articulate listener as a leader, meetings can drag on forever. At work, you may have little control over meetings, but in your private life, you can learn to avoid or minimize the time-gobbling aspects of meetings. Here are some of your options, depending on whether you are an active participant or merely an observer:

Use Patterning

Instead of using an agenda in the traditional outline form, try printing your major topics across a blackboard. Then as people suggest ideas, add them to the major topics in patterning form. For example, at a meeting of our co-op food store, the discussion of a new location was hotly debated. The patterning began as:

and as each opinion and report was voiced, the pattern became:

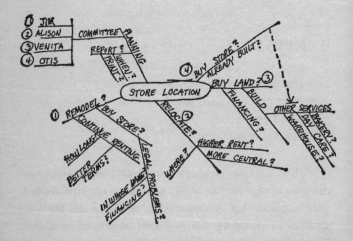

No suggestions were shouted down and lost; the ideas

were more important than the personalities; and each participant had an overall view during the meeting of where the suggestion fit into the central idea.

In every meeting there are people who wander off the track, start discussing last month's vacation, tell pointless and long-winded stories. If you are in charge, don't be afraid to interrupt to ask politely, "Where does this fit into our discussion?" The time you save for everyone will be appreciated.

Attend For a Limited Length of Time

Tell the person in charge you can only stay for one hour. Usually the important topics will then be covered more briskly and all you will miss will be the chitchat at the end.

Don't Go

There are many many people who contribute much time and large talents directly, and who also refuse to go to any meetings. When asked to help an organization, don't be afraid to say, "I'd be happy to help twice a month (or whatever), but I can't come to any meetings. What, specifically, can I do?"

Keep Your Hands Busy

For those meetings at which you are primarily an observer than a participant (such as city council meetings), take along something to do with your hands. It's a great time to practice sketching, for example, or just inspired doodling (if you think you can't draw, see the Nicholaides book mentioned on the Reading List at the end of Part

Two). And, of course, all the needle arts (except machine embroidery) are perfect for boring meetings.

9. WAITING

- Expect to wait and be prepared
- Relax, observe, enjoy

Some feel modern life is nothing *but* waiting—for trains, doctors, stoplights, appointments, paychecks, acceptances, births, death. Your attitude about waiting usually reveals more about your feelings about time than any other item on this list.

If waiting is something that makes you livid, you probably suffer from more than merely our common unconscious cultural perception of time (see Part Four: Perspectives).

A slight change in attitude and some preplanning can remove much of the unpleasantness of waiting.

Expect To Wait and Be Prepared

In most early cultures men and women carried fleece and a spindle in their sleeves or packs. They were never too busy to stop and chat with someone because as they talked, everyone spun thread for weaving and embroidery.

If you carry a pleasant diversion with you—needlework, a camera, a book, a sketch pad and pen—you never mind waiting. Instead, you feel like you've been given the gift of a few extra free minutes a day. And these little five- or fifteen-minute waits can add up.

Relax, Observe, Enjoy

There is no need to fill every minute of every day with busy activities. If you find yourself waiting for fifteen minutes, you don't *have* to read or sketch or stitch. You can give yourself permission to sit and enjoy the quiet, watch other people, eavesdrop, daydream, or just plain vegetate.

Unfortunately, people who are bothered by waiting are usually too tense to do this. Recent research has found that tense people can't even identify which parts of their bodies are tense; this makes relaxing difficult unless it is practiced. Use your waiting time to perfect relaxation techniques such as this one:

1. Tense every muscle in your body—eyebrows, jaws, lips, neck, chest, arms, hands, buttocks, thighs, calves, and toes—for a slow count of 10.
2. Relax everything for a slow count of 10.
3. Tense everything even harder for a slow count of 10.
4. Relax everything for a slow count of 10.
5. Hardest of all, tense—and then relax for a slow count of 10.
6. Now imagine thick, viscous warm water is being poured on your head. Feel it ooze slowly and pleasantly downward, easing every muscle tension as it passes. Any muscle that is tense acts as a dam to the water, until you make that muscle

relax. Relax it by tightening first and then relaxing the muscle.

If you are relaxed and you are still waiting, try some deep breathing. With your mouth closed, breathe in through your nose until your belly bulges out (but not uncomfortable). Expel the air through your nose by deflating your belly. That's all there is to it. (Many of us were incorrectly taught to suck in our bellies at the same time we breathe in deeply. This is back ass-ward. Your belly should fill with air like a balloon as you breathe in.)

Once you are relaxed, you can truly enjoy the world around you—the smells, the sounds, the patterns of light, the textures, the colors, the oddities, the humor.

10. MENTAL BLOCKS

- Confront mental blocks directly
- Take one step
- Ask for help
- Wait

Three months ago I said I'd paint some trim strips for our daughter's new bedroom. To this day, the trim is unpainted. Every day I think how I'm still not painting the trim, but that thought doesn't make me pick up the paintbrush. I have a major mental block about painting that trim. Why? For the same reason you have mental blocks: because it's something I have to do and don't want to. There are much fancier ways of saying that, but they don't say more.

But it doesn't do any good to examine why you have mental blocks if it doesn't remove the mental block itself. And having mental blocks often destroys your use of free time. You can't justify starting something on your Wish list with an unfinished task staring you in the face. You begin to feel guilty and frustrated and angry all at once, which interferes with your enjoyment of your time by effectively paralyzing you. So how can we remove those mental blocks?

A modest beginning is to change our image of the mental block. Do you visualize it as an impenetrable wall across your path? If so, you are apt to have hopeless feelings about your mental blocks; they'll never go away and there's no way to get around them. Try visualizing your mental blocks as *blocks*, three-dimensional cubes in the middle of your path. They're inconvenient and they stand in the way, but your choices in dealing with them are to go around them, to go over them, or to nudge them little by little out of the way. Only the very strong feel confident enough to walk through them.

We've all had mental blocks in our lives; here's how others deal with them.

Confront Mental Blocks Directly

Start either by saying out loud or by writing down, "I have a giant mental block about painting the trim" (only put your own mental block in there). If you know why you have the block, say or write down that too: "It's a stupid job and I hate cleaning brushes and of all the hundreds of things I *have* to do, that one is least appealing. And anyway, how did I get roped into this job? You're the trim painter in this family, not me." Be as petty and unfair as you wish (no matter, for example, that I initially volunteered to paint trim).

Many people are not even aware of their mental blocks; all they are aware of is a vague queasy feeling that something is wrong, that something is not getting done that should be done. As writers, we daily hear people of all ages sigh, "Someday I'd like to be a writer—if I could only find the time." Hard fact: you'll never have more time than you have today. Time isn't the problem; it's the mental block about writing, caused by fear of failure and other fears.

Robbie put off writing her first juvenile novel for years, finding many ways to fill each day so that when the nagging thought periodically surfaced—*"someday* I'm gonna write that novel"—she could always claim there was not time. Then one day she confronted this mental block by writing about it. "What am I afraid of?" she wrote. "There are so many unanswered questions in my story, like can a 13-year-old girl really affect a 78-year-old?'' Suddenly, the fear of failure disappeared. It didn't matter if the writing was good or bad; that judgment could come much later. All that mattered was starting to write the novel. And funny, she was as busy as she'd ever been, but she still squeezed out enough time to finish the novel. Granted, it took two years of short writing stints, sometimes only a sentence a week. But the novel was written, and finishing it was a truly glorious feeling.

You may not care at all about writing a novel, but you'll be on the way to the same glorious feeling when you confront your own mental blocks directly.

Confronting your mental blocks means nothing unless you take the first step to remove them. Read on.

Take One Step

Mental blocks are a form of inertia. To overcome that inertia takes but a small bit of energy, after which a rolling momentum builds and you are usually able to complete the task, to set aside the mental block. And the intense relief that follows feels great; not only did you accomplish something and overcome a block, but *you* did it.

So the first step is to break the mental block down into manageable portions. Write down or say out loud all the steps you must take to complete whatever's annoying you.

Take that stupid trim I haven't painted. My steps are: set up the sawhorses, find the paint in the godawful mess called a garage, get a paintbrush that isn't stiff or ruined, paint, clean brush, put away paint and brush, put away trim when dry.

Now for five minutes only, right now, before you read another word, take the first step on *your* list. This second, do it! There, I put the stupid trim out back on the saw-horses. And amazing—if I could have found the paint in the godawful mess called a garage, I would have painted it right then.

Once you've removed mental blocks from the fuzzy neb-ulous regions of the brain and taken the first step toward dealing with them, it's like knocking the first domino down—the rest follows in a whoosh.

Often mental blocks have been lurking for years, caus-ing ridiculous delays in living. Have you arranged it so you can't deal with a mental block until you do some-thing else first and you can't do that until you do this and you can't do this because . . . on and on and on? Read about Trivia as a time-gobbler in the beginning of Part Three.

Ask For Help

Two people nudging a mental block can move it easier than one. Ask for help, not necessarily to complete the task, but to take the first step. Someone who helps you remove a mental block is a treasured friend.

Our friend bought an old house cheaply, but it needed work in every room to make it livable. Every time he thought about the amount of work, he went into a cata-tonic fir (watched TV all weekend). Meanwhile, the fric-tion level in the house reached an all-time high, as his wife screamed every time she looked at the peeling wallpaper and dingy, rotted windows. Finally the friend asked us for help. In one weekend, the four of us peeled off all the wallpaper and replaced the windows. Now they've repainted the walls and trim and have one room in the house they can stand to sit in. In exchange, they helped us to finish our daughter's new bedroom (I should have asked them to paint the trim).

Ask for help. And give it, too.

Wait

Sometimes your mental blocks are more than not wanting to do something you have to do. Sometimes your basic good sense is warning you that it's too soon, that you haven't found the best solution to your mental block problem. There's probably a better way that you can't see yet.

We live in a small one-bedroom house. For seven years our daughter slept in an oversized closet off our bedroom, and for seven years we knew we had to find a different way before she became bigger than the room. Over the years we came up with dozens of ways to rearrange the house, all of which involved bad ideas, too much work, and too much money for supplies. Over the years Tony began to develop a mental block about making the bedroom. He kept putting it off and putting it off.

Then one day he realized that by dropping a wall in the uncesessarily large dining room, we'd have a large bedroom for our daughter. The mental block was finally nudged out of his path. Two weeks later, we had our bedroom

If Tony had acted on any of the earlier ideas, we'd

have had an imperfect solution to our problem. But when the best idea presented itself, he knew it immediately.

To be outwitted, some mental blocks must be outwaited.

Ten Human Tools for
Managing Time

A story

Once there was a little gray rat who skittered and scurried all day long. Exactly what he did is not remembered, but he did look extremely busy all the time. His right forepaw always took a stitch in time; his left perpetually slapped the right to remind it that haste makes waste; one eye was fixed forever ahead of him while the other watched behind; his hind paws juggled a schedule and a watch back and forth; and his tail—why, his tail twitched uncontrollably.

If he had nothing else to do, he leaped onto the exercise wheel for a second or two. Every night before he fell asleep—if he did—he planned his next day down to the second. In his sleep he mumbled, "They all depend on me." His wife could never figure out who he was talking about.

When the little gray rat inevitably dropped dead of a heart attack, the coroner wrote, "Hurry poisoning." The rat's family was sad to see him go, of course, and so were his friends, both of them. But they each breathed a sigh of relief when no one else was looking; being around a little gray rat can wear you down.

But that wasn't the end of it. The little gray rat had specified that his headstone read "Efficient." The unappreciative stonecutter substituted "Dead."

THE END

The time-gobblers were tied into Downers in your Upper/Downer pattern. The remedy in each case was to disengage and de-synch from them or to modify them to your satisfaction. Negative solutions for negative situations: the best you could do is break a bad habit, yours or someone else's.

Now we turn away from Downers, to your Wish list and the Presumé you've forgotten.

Here are some useful tools for getting those things done in a human way. They are tools, instead of rules, because you don't need another "should" in your life, though our language often makes it impossible to avoid the word.

Please accept them as offered, as tools—not as slogans removing the need to think, not as inflexible imperatives or rules, not even necessarily as principles of action; there are times, for each of these tools, when it is exactly the wrong thing to do.

These are soft tools, suitable for work on living human beings. They are ideas to work with to support an attitude: that enjoying what you do is far more important than doing more, or doing it faster.

So use them. But don't think you can or should live by them or any other rules. Only little gray rats do that.

1. AIM TO FEEL GOOD, NOT TO DO MORE

One of the ironies of time management, whether it's personal or mercantile or industrial, is that the harried person usually is convinced that he has to do more, especially if he already has too much to do. And the habitually harried person goes further: he arranges to have too much to do.

Our prime human tool of time management attacks this problem.

Back in Part One: Action, your "do-it-now" exercise proved to you what you already know: that your feelings about using time are totally subjective. When you feel good about yourself, you couldn't care less whether you get everything done or merely one little thing. When you feel bad about yourself, it doesn't change that feeling even if you do get everything done.

Remember this, periodically. Rather than asking yourself whether you are making good, efficient, or effective use of the current moment, ask yourself instead, "Do I find this satisfying?'' Make that a habit, and you are asking the question, ''Is the life I'm leading satisfying me?'' Notice that there is no permanent answer; the quality of your life changes constantly. Only you can judge if that quality is good, and if not, only you can improve it. But pumping your time full of more activities cannot improve it, unless those activities increase your satisfaction.

How do you improve the quality of your life? This is where your uniqueness comes in: you must start, like everyone else, by ensuring that your human needs are satisfied (we discussed some of them in Part Two: Pause); but you have other wants and needs. Part One: Action suggested tools and tricks for ferreting them out, but that was only a beginning. It's an ongoing process.

How do you apply this tool to managing your personal time? Like all good human tools, this one provides no answer; it merely poses an important question which you can answer according to your situation. Use it by asking yourself the question when you need to do it.

There's another formulation of the same question, which we have avoided up to now lest we be mistaken for sounding Cosmic: the next time you feel harried, driven, rushed, overloaded, or fragmented; whenever you feel there is so much to do that you'll never get it all done; when the list gets too long, don't ask ''How can I get it all done?'' Ask instead, ''Why am I doing this?''

2. REMEMBER THAT YOU'RE IN CHARGE

There are so many choices available to us—which job, where to live, what to buy, who to see, what to be—that it is all too easy to let the prospect of making these choices inundate us, until we feel we're drowning. The next step is to say to yourself, "Look, I'm drowning, so I just don't have time to enjoy myself." Like it or not, by not being in charge of your choices, you have made a choice by default: to drown.

Remember, you're in charge. You don't have to drown. Not only that, you're the only one who can keep yourself from drowning, because there aren't any lifeguards out there who will rescue you.

You have gradually set life up to be the way it is now, and you can gradually change it to be the way you want.

Perhaps your reply is, "I wish I could just stop, but so many people depend on me."

How true is this statement? Not very.

Usually the person who thinks he is so indispensable is fooling himself. Naturally, we all want to be needed and important, but in truth, the world can and will get along without us someday. If you think everybody depends on you, then you have engineered that false situation, and you can engineer yourself out of it, if you really want to.

The human tool of remembering you're in charge helps you when at last you realize that the binds and double binds you're in come ultimately from yourself.

The Upper/Downer pattern you made is your clue to those situations over which you must take charge. If, for example, chauffeuring your kids is the most hateful among your Downers, take charge: either take measures to cut down on chauffeuring (such as buying them bikes, saying "no," telling them they're responsible for their own transportation) or take responsibility for not changing the situation: "I choose to drive myself crazy chauffeuring the kids around."

A prayer attributed to St. Francis of Assisi, when correctly interpreted, is another statement of this tool of time management: "Help me to change what I can change, to accept what I cannot change, and to know the difference." Some people emphasize the second part and use this prayer to justify a cop-out to fatalism. But the first and third parts lead to satisfaction, and there are a lot more things we can change than we allow ourselves to think.

It's your time. You are in charge of it. Your choices make the difference. And no one else really cares.

3. DEFEND PEAK PERIODS

Within the past two decades there has been yet another scientific revolution in understanding why we act the way we do: we now know that much of what we do is dictated or modified by territorial behavior. In *African Genesis* and other books, Robert Ardrey summarized a half-century's anthropological work on the territoriality of animals and man.

Briefly, an animal behaves as if a certain territory belongs to him and defends it against all comers in his species. A territorial animal is nearly invincible in its own territory; but even against an opponent which it has just repulsed on its own territory, it will invariably be defeated on the opponent's territory. The size of the territory depends on the species of animal, with territories of a few square yards sufficing for some bird and rodent species, while lions and bears have territories of many square miles. A territory may be patrolled by a single family, or by an extended group in case of social animals like lions or primates.

The territorial urge is very strong. In some animals it is stronger than the urge to protect offspring, the urge to mate, and the urge to feed. Among birds, where territoriality is pronounced, it has even been observed that no mating takes place unless the male has first established his territory.

Territoriality casts new light on certain observations of human behavior: a man feels that his home is his castle (and reacts powerfully to defend it); you are at a disadvantage when you argue with your boss in his office (instead of yours); and in athletic contests, you can usually bet on the home team winning. Human beings defend their territories, and it makes them stronger.

The same thing happens when you defend your time; it makes you stronger, and you seem to get more done more satisfactorily in the defended period.

Now, you can no more defend *all* your time than a single lion can defend all of Africa.

Assuming that you have little control over how you spend your work hours, it is your personal or free time that needs defending. And within those few hours, you have small peaks and valleys of energy. The peaks are most worth defending. For example, when you have driven home in heavy freeway traffic after a stress-filled day of work, you hit the living room drained of energy. That is not the best time to draw, paint, write, make love, or do any of the special things on your Wish list.

Nor is immediately after a heavy dinner a good time, because your body's using oxygen to digest the food and it doesn't have a lot of oxygen left over for thinking or moving; after you've been drinking is not a good time, either, if it wipes you out. How badly do you want to get started on something that is fun and satisfying? You might consider changing your evening habits: exercise when you come home so you will have more stamina; eat your day's heavy meal at noon or late at night; cut back on or eliminate evening drinks.

But maybe an hour after you've come home and rested, maybe eaten, maybe run or bicycled for twenty minutes, you feel slightly rejuvenated. Build on that moment! This is not the time to do idiot work like cleaning or watching the tube or chatting on the phone with someone you don't like very much. This is when you can start chipping away at your Wish list.

When are your peaks, and how do you find out?

Relaxed observation over a week's time will tell you all you need to know. Check your moods, your energy level, your sleepy times. But don't turn this, too, into a task. We once explained the physiological correlates of peak periods (your body temperature rises) to a tense and intense woman, who then insisted on carrying around with her a chart and a rectal thermometer! Relaxed observation is enough.

And if you are always too tired to do anything, you might consider (1) having a doctor's physical to see if anything's wrong; and (2) starting a modest exercise program, such as swimming or running three times a week. Your body's giving you as clear a message as it can: give me more oxygen. (Review how to set up a physical exercise program discussed in Part Two: Pause.)

All of this preparation for your peak period of energy goes down the drain if you allow yourself to be diverted from it by a phone call or any other interruption. You must learn to defend your peak periods by saying, "I'm busy— don't bother me right now" on those nights when you are doing something for yourself. (See Ten Time-Gobblers and How to Starve Them.)

During the week, choose two or three peak periods for

doing something on your Wish list, but make sure that you also have occasional times set aside when you don't have to do anything, even something on your Wish list. These periods are most worth defending and the hardest to actually defend, but you can learn with practice. Defend them like crazy until it becomes an easy habit.

Weekends are different. Having a whole day to yourself, not subject to an employer's clock, gives you a chance to see what your true natural rhythms are. Do you wake up early, instantly alert, or are you a late sleeper, slow to function? Do you need a short nap in the afternoon or do you steam ahead until bedtime? Do you conk out early or do you love to work half the night?

When you're a child, it seems that one of the payoffs of being adult is to do whatever you want whenever you want. But a college professor relative had to wait for retirement to fit himself to his natural rhythm of staying up all night and sleeping during the day. He now works in his darkroom, reads, writes letters, and happily putters around the house while the rest of his family is snoring. He sleeps all morning, catnaps in the afternoon, and still spends more time with his children and grandchildren than anyone else we know.

What are your natural rhythms? Weekends are your chance to override the artificial hours of the work week. If, for example, you sleep late every weekend when you are a natural early riser, you may feel too sluggish to do anything for yourself all weekend. On the other hand, if you prefer to work late at night and you're always booked for an evening out Saturday nights, you're going to continue to feel frustrated about never getting anything done.

One solution is to give yourself permission to do something for yourself from time to time, say once a month.

Prepare ahead of time to defend your peaks, and it's much easier. For example, one of our students had taken twenty rolls of color slides on a trip to Peru and kept *not* reviewing them to pick out the best. The idea of viewing 700 slides was overwhelming to him, and he felt he needed several uninterrupted hours for it. The only time he had free was Saturday nights, which were peak periods for him, but he and his wife always went to one or another relative's house that night. He finally chose one Saturday night for himself and wrote on his calendar, "slide viewing." Then when he was invited for an evening, he looked at his calendar and said, "I'm sorry, but I can't come that Saturday. How about the following week?"

The difficulty in this tool of time management is that your peak periods of energy and your mate's may not mesh. It is not always easy to reconcile these differences, but if you wish to be undisturbed during your peak periods, you must learn to respect your mate's. (See Learn To Live As a Couple at the end of Part Three.)

4. MAKE TIME TO MAKE MORE TIME

Sometimes we cannot avoid planning and scheduling personal time. Sometimes we need to elbow aside some activities so that we'll have time to do what we want.

Some "time experts" advise you to start each day making a list of what you want to do that day, or to end each day planning the next. If this approach really *works* for you and you feel good about your use of time without feeling harried and frazzled, then by all means use it. But this kind of nonstop scheduling is what drove most of us nuts in the first place.

Planning and setting priorities and scheduling cannot be transferred over from industrial management to your personal life—unless you want your life more factory-like, that is. We all know mothers who try to run their families like a Detroit production line, and they succeed. They are uniformly frazzled and frustrated, and there are strikes from the children and walkouts by the husbands.

Instead of planning your time every day, plan only when you are bothered by what you're not getting done. Sometimes this means planning twice a day and sometimes once a week or once a month or even less often.

When you have to plan, use the patterning technique you've learned in the Action section to plan what you want to get done, as well as what you have to get done. It gives you an overview of what you want to get done without putting an automatic time value or priority on everything, and this is crucial. Often our most pleasant activities, such as playing with our children, reading a good book, and going for a walk, do not have a time value at all. We just *do* them and keep doing them until we're done, whether it takes five minutes or seventeen years. If we were to impose a time schedule on these activities, we'd deprive ourselves of some of the magic of being human.

For example, a student of ours, a divorced father, wanted to spend more time with his children, so he put that on his Wish list and added it to the father role on his Life pattern. Then he sat down to schedule time with his kids. We advised him to schedule his other activities so that he could free up such times, but to stay loose. If he had scheduled his day hour by hour, you can bet that during the time he had scheduled as "Spending Time With Children," they would not have been the least bit interested in spending time with him; if he had scheduled his time according to priorities, he probably would not have set "Spending Time With Children" as a high priority.

Important parts of being human should not be scheduled at all.

Make time to make more time, but for the things in life that really count.

5. PATTERN YOUR LISTS

When you need to plan your time, use patterning for an overall view of what needs doing, instead of bogging down in making lists.

It's late Thursday evening. You've been running around all week, working late, coming home too late and too pooped to do anything. You feel mad and frazzled and depressed and dissatisfied. You haven't done the dishes for three days. Your apartment looks like the aftermath of a commando raid. You'll be gone tomorrow night and all day Saturday. Sunday is Mother's Day. Your mother expects a feast here. How are you going to get it all done? And be human on Monday?

What exactly needs to be done? There's so much, you don't know where to start. Dinner—she has a fit if you take her to a restaurant ("Isn't right," she says)—what can you make that doesn't take time?

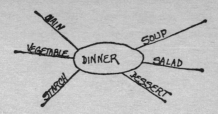

Now to plan dishes that don't take forever or can be made ahead or are do-it-yourself by each person. Aha! That lettuce soup is simple and you can make it Saturday night before going out.

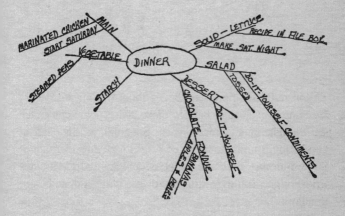

There, the menu is done and you can make a shopping list (and if you're really organized, you'll do it by aisles in the grocery store). Now to make a patterned list for your post-hurricane apartment.

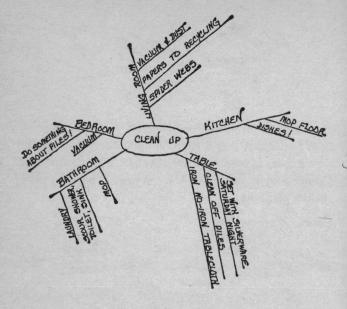

You're beginning to feel better about what needs doing. It seems manageable, but oh, those dishes—you can't face the thought of all those dishes. So don't do them all at once. Do 15 minutes worth of dishes now and 15 minutes in the morning while the coffee is brewing and 15 minutes Friday night. Little by little, the dishes will get done before Sunday.

Patterned lists work better than linear lists because in one glance you can get an overall grasp of what needs doing, and because you don't have to worry about order, priority, or sequencing while you pattern. Later, you can underline or star, preferably in a second color, the activities that are time-related. For example, one of our current lists looks like this:

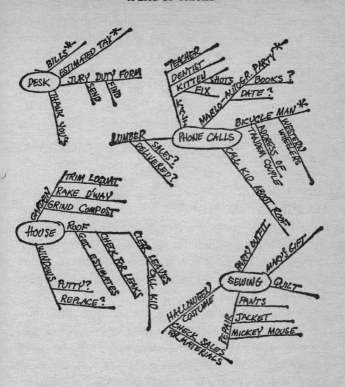

Under Phone Calls, the Bicycle Man is starred because we said we'd call him between 10 and 11:30 AM. Under Desk, the bills are starred because they're due in two days.

We keep our patterned list posted on the kitchen bulletin board, crossing off what gets done, adding new activities and categories as needed. When the list gets unreadable, we make a new one. But eventually, everything on the list gets done, even if it takes a long time to get around to doing it.

The only danger in making these lists is that you'll forget what really counts: the Wish list you made earlier. You could easily spend all your time washing bathroom walls and never get around to learning to fly (and we've never met anyone who got their jollies from washing bathroom walls). Since your Wish list is very private, you won't want to post it for all the world to see. But look at it from time to time to keep yourself on track. Make sure you're doing a little something for yourself every day and not bogging down in the trivial time-consuming activities, which you can pattern out of your way.

6. PILE AND FILE

Patterned lists are helpful for organizing your activities, but to juggle the Things in your life, the possessions that tend to clump up and sprawl into messes, learn to make piles as you go.

We have a friend who wanted to socialize more since her divorce, but her continuing excuse for not inviting people over was that her dining room table, her only work surface, was junked up with too many things. Occasionally she worked her way down close to the surface of the table, but new possessions soon stacked up again. (We suggested she give a buffet from the floor and forget the table, but she hated to look at the mess on the table and was certain that visitors would too.) After she got over her real problem—fear of interacting again as a "single" woman—she quickly cleared the table. Instead of picking one object at a time off the top and trying to decide what to do with it, she concentrated only on sorting the contents of her messy table into piles according to category or function. Then she attacked the piles, one by one, working away at them until she bought, made, or arranged storage space for everything that she truly needed to keep. (And now our friend has people over so often we never see her anymore).

Trying to find something in the midst of a mess is aggravating and takes time you could use enjoying yourself. There's no stopping Things. They circulate, almost with a life of their own. The trick is to set it up so that you can capture your possessions as they flow past you: a place for everything and everything in piles ready to go to its place.

Trouble, however, usually arises when we have not found a place for something; then the offending Thing is shifted around from one surface to the next, one room to another. In order to deal with the daily flow of possessions, you must have adequate storage for all types of possessions: papers, hobby materials, clothing, books, toys, tools, and gadgets. So the next time you are cleaning up a mess equivalent to our friend's table, keep a pencil and paper nearby and jot down the things you own that do not have a resting place. Consult Tools of Organization on page 207 for ideas on storage systems and then spend the time and money on buying, making, or arranging what you need.

Better yet, train yourself to pile and file as you go. For example, mail can be a problem, both at home and at work. The same procedure is useful in both places. Open your mail at your desk (which at home could be as small as a drawer in the kitchen). Immediately throw away the uninteresting junk. Open the bills, gasp, write a reminder on your calendar three days before the due dates, and put the bills in your bill file. (Files and piles are practically interchangeable; files are for thinner things.) Read the personal letters and either answer them immediately or put them in the "To Be Answered" file. Write a reminder on your calendar to answer those letters. For impersonal letters of the can-you-help-our-organization kind, answer at the bottom of the letter and return immediately. For events you might possibly attend, pin the flyer on the bulletin board and write yourself a reminder on the calendar to think about it later. You can decide then whether to go. Read the newspapers, underline important dates, make notes on your calendar to call people, and throw away or file the newsletters. Put magazines beside your bed, favorite chair, or in the bathroom for later reading.

Files should be set up in broad categories rather than many picky topics. If you save articles people send you, don't make a separate folder for each one. Put those that are appropriate to categories you already have (say, Tools or Plants or Needlework) in the correct files and the rest in a general ''Articles'' folder.

Inevitably when you are dispatching into piles, you sort down to the last little batch of doodads, which fit into no piles at all. If you can bear it, throw them away; otherwise, they'll continue to plague you every time you clean up. If you're a true pack rat, though, you won't be able to part with those screws and nails and switches and swatches because you'll say, ''I might need them someday.'' So keep one drawer in the kitchen or one shoe box at the back of the closet for these odds and ends. When the drawer overflows, it's time to make piles again, this time more hardheadedly.

If you find the same types of possessions junking up repeatedly, you should examine your storage system. Is it in the best location? Does it mesh with your behavior? Set it up so that you don't cause yourself extra work. Keep your calendar, files, notebooks, wastebasket, and bill drawer close together and then open your mail there. If you always open the mail in your favorite living room chair and your files are in the kitchen, move your files next to the chair.

Be certain that making piles to organize your possessions is a time-saver for you, not a time-waster. You should only sort if the mess bothers you or prevents you from enjoying yourself.

Tony's workbench in the garage looks like somebody upended five toolboxes on it and then emptied a garbage can on top of that. Throughout the years Robbie has tried to help him organize the mess, suggesting that he hang all his tools with the outline of each tool painted in bright colors on the wall; spending hours on weekends helping him through the layers, making piles; and setting up dishpans labeled Electrical, Nails, and Screws, so that he could easily make piles as he works. He still works by tossing every tool, rag, nail, piece of sandpaper, and apple core in the general direction of his long workbench. He whistles while he works—usually outside, on a makeshift work surface laid on sawhorses. One day he said, "You know what I've discovered? That mess doesn't bother me." So he doesn't worry about it any more. Our only problem comes when Robbie wants to find a tool, so we've set her up with her own simple toolbox, organized in a way that suits her "neatnik" behavior patterns. And Tony is willing to shuffle through the compost heap on top of the workbench whenever Robbie needs a more specialized tool that isn't in her toolbox.

7. UNLOAD; SAY "NO"

Busy executives who intend to remain alive awhile learn to delegate responsibility. In business, this works because the boss has the clout to ensure that delegated tasks get done. Our personal lives aren't structured in quite the same way, but we can still use the satisfying part of delegating: we can unload.

We can unload in three directions: to other people, to devices that do tasks better and more painlessly, and into the Great Vacuum.

Often you take on a responsibility which is properly someone else's (usually for such reasons as the dubious pleasure of martyrdom or for gratitude). For example, your kids do not need everything done for them. They can and must learn, little by little, to dress themselves, pack their own lunches, get to school on time, make arrangements for overnights, fold their own laundry, wash their own hair, cook, wash dishes, and help with chores around the house. If you continue to take on these responsibilities, feeling frazzled and harried, with little time for yourself, it's your own fault.

Another friend was Supermom for nineteen years. She did everything a good Supermom should for her kids: drove them to lessons, cleverly decorated their rooms, served on PTA committees, and staged elaborate birthday parties every year with homemade cakes in the shape of circus tents, footballs, and kangaroos. She spent hours scrubbing her house, making everyone's clothes, baking cookies, being a den mother and Bluebird leader. She also fussed and fretted and felt frazzled and harried and unappreciated. After nineteen years of this—and in no small part because of this—her marriage fell apart, her kids left home with a portion of her bitterness, and she had to find a paying job for the first time in her life. "You know what my son remembers? Not the circus-tent cake or the clean house. He remembers the little yellow raincoat we bought together at a Goodwill store when he was six and the walk home in the rain.'' Burdens you take on are remembered by no one but yourself.

Unloading means handing a specific job over to the person to whom it belongs, and then letting go. If you delegate dressing herself to your seven-year-old daughter, you must accept the consequences gracefully. Some days she'll choose clothes you approve of; on others, she'll choose a pink shirt with one red knee sock and one white knee sock (''because mixed together, they make pink''). If you unload on your mate the responsibility of folding his socks and underwear, you can't allow yourself to be upset when he stands back and practices dunk shots at the sock drawer. And if your mate unloads responsibility on you for building your own storage systems, he should not be overly upset with your crooked shelves and rickety boxes. (In our house we unload a lot.)

Some jobs and responsibilities do not clearly belong to any one person. Some of those that you take on can cause you to grumble and growl, and would be better unloaded on someone else. However, unload on other people with a liberal dose of consideration, and be sure to reciprocate. No one wants to take over all of someone else's nuisances.

And be honest when someone tries to unload on you, when you're less than enthusiastic about the job yourself. Of course there are some unpleasant things you do for others out of love, but hidden resentment is dangerous. And if you don't bring it out into the open, it's your own fault.

On a simpler level, you can unload worrying about appointments to a kitchen timer. Say you have to catch a bus in 45 minutes and you want to finish reading a novel first. You could easily jump up every five minutes to check the clock and not enjoy your novel at all. But if you unload the worry to the kitchen timer, setting it to ring in 35 minutes, you'll enjoy reading twice as much as you would if you were fussing over the clock.

Many of the activities that feel like obligations—especially the ones you've taken on yourself—don't need to be done at all. (The Supermom of our example learned this far too late.) These can be jettisoned. Ask yourself, "Would the world go on if I didn't do this?" If the answer is "yes," unload that activity into the Great Vacuum.

With a little practice in unloading, you begin to anticipate the situations *before* you are forced to unload them. It's called saying "no."

Because of polite upbringing, some of us were trained to be Nice. For us, it is painful to say "no" to anybody, and we can't do it without girding ourselves and shaking after. If people always make you offers you can't refuse because you're Nice, learn to say "I'll call you later with an answer. I have to check my calendar (or with my husband or wife)." Then practice saying "no" to yourself until you can call back and refuse. You, too, can say "no" to endless and pointless meetings, to idle phone talk, to going places where you don't want to be, accompanied by people you'd rather not be with. Instead of stopping for a drink after work with the office bore, you can say, "No thanks, I'm in training for a marathon."

Too often what glops up our free time, preventing us from doing what's important to us, is trivial, silly, or a real time-gobbler. For example, we recently had lunch with another busy author. It hadn't been easy to set up a day convenient for all of us, and when we met in the restaurant, we had only an hour together. But as we began to catch up on old times, a young lady, all painted and frilled, appeared at the table.

"Hi, I'm Penny," she breezed, "and this is the Wednesday fashion show from the Stupid Little Boutique next door. The dress I have on is made of . . ."

"Excuse me," Robbie interrupted, reasonably. "Does anyone here want to hear this? I, for one, am not in the least bit interested." The model moved on. If we had not stopped the babbling model, we would have allowed one hour together to be shortened by a sales pitch we didn't want to hear.

8. DO IT NOW!

For the small, niggling annoyances that build into major headaches if ignored, there is no finer tool than "Do it now!"

Apply it when you feel a little twinge of irritation about some little task. When, for example, your child has left sneakers in the bathroom doorway, put them where they belong (under his pillow) rather than tripping over them all day until he comes home from his soccer game (at which time you can still explain to him how he disturbed the order of the universe). If, every time you fix dinner, you grumble about how scummy the wall next to the stove has gotten, clean it right then.

Learn to apply this delicate tool of time management only to small things, or your life could become more harried, and your time more fragmented. Skittering from one activity to another is more than a symptom of faulty time management, it is one of its chief contributing causes.

But when the remedy for a pint-sized irritation is direct and small,

DO IT NOW!

9. SAY "YES" TO LIFE

Once we were backpacking along the John Muir trail in California's spectacular High Sierra, soaking up sun, breezes, and fresh air at the top of a mountain pass. We had seen only four people in as many days. Looking ahead, we watched a figure grow larger and larger as it climbed up the trail toward us. A man with an enormous pack on his back jogged closer, his eyebrows furrowed.

"Hello," we called. "Where are you headed?" "Can't stop," he gasped and whizzed by. He was *running*.

"Do you have to be somewhere soon?" we shouted at his back.

"No-o-o," and he disappeared around a corner.

Perhaps he enjoyed running the trail and the running was more satisfying to him than his surroundings. Perhaps you enjoy running your trail, too. But for most of us, filling our time with hurry-hurry-hurry activities leaves us torn and fragmented, uneasy and unhappy. Yet when we add even a small bit of sparkle, of enjoyment, spontaneity, or relaxation to our day, we may still have the same amount of work to do, but because we feel more calm and peaceful, it's manageable. We may not get it all done, but we don't care.

How can you say "yes" to life? It's not something that can be scheduled or planned for. You can't say, "I will work until 6 PM and then I will laugh, sparkle, and feel loved until 7." It doesn't work that way. Many of life's best experiences and feelings are elusive and transitory and can't be planned for, or stored up in a bank like money. You have to act on them at the moment they occur. If you are running through life, you may be moving too fast to notice them.

The people who complain of never getting anything done also sigh that they haven't had time to take advantage of the good things all around them. What could be more back assward? Say "yes" to the good things in life *first* so that your life will be so rich in experiences and feelings that you'll be satisfied with what you do accomplish and not worried about what you don't get done.

10. STRETCH AND STAY FLEXIBLE

Your legs may be so strong that you can beat a kangaroo at leg wrestling, but unless they're limber and flexible, you can lame yourself jogging around the block. Many would-be runners have quit permanently because they refused to take the time for loosening-up exercises, ran anyhow, and injured themselves. Professional athletes such as football players wouldn't dare skip pregame warm-up stretches, because they know that unless they're loose, they're very injury-prone.

The same is true of your expectations. They can be strong and suitable, but seek them inflexibly and you're bound to injure yourself. This book has helped you focus on what you want to get done and how to do it. Your expectations are undoubtedly at an all-time high. Beware.

If you had only yourself to watch over, you'd have few problems managing your time. But you don't have only yourself; there are those who live with you, your neighbors, your co-workers, and a whole crowd of people you meet only now and then. They all have expectations and things to get done, and theirs don't always jibe with yours.

Be as flexible as you can. Try not to blow your stack when your plans are inevitably interrupted or sidetracked. Ask yourself whether, in the greater scheme of life, it really matters that you can't do *today* what you'd planned to do today.

Disappointments and frustrations are inevitable, but you can rob them of their sting by practicing an attitude of flexibility.

HOW TO KEEP YOUR TOOLS SHARP

The tools of time management, like any tools, wear down with use. You could avoid this by not using them, but then they're useless as tools. Better keep your tools sharp.

1. Use them carefully, and only for their intended use.
2. Use them to build other tools, more suitable to your applications.
3. Use them wisely, but know that tools wear out and must be eventually replaced by better tools.

Ten Time-Stretchers

Now that you've thought about the way you've chosen to live your life, examined how you may have boxed yourself into corners, taken some modest steps toward eliminating some time-drags, and considered some useful human tools for managing your time, make use of these time-stretchers:

1. COOPERATION

Despite headlines about graft, publicly unethical politicians, robber barons, and gangsters, the real American way has always been cooperation. Since the first, we've helped ourselves by helping our neighbors.

Today in the cities a lot of that sense of sharing and cooperation has gone, to be replaced by mistrust and paranoia. We'd help our neighbors if only our neighbors weren't such creeps. He borrows tools and doesn't return them; she leaves her kids with us and never reciprocates; they aren't fair about doing their share; they voted for What's-His-Face? And besides, we're afraid of them. There are problems in cooperation; there are problems in anything involving people. But a growing number of Americans are interested in living well together by helping each other.

You, too, can enrich your life and "save" time by cooperating, on whatever scale you choose. There are food co-ops, babysitting co-ops, nursery school co-ops, yarn and fabric co-ops, tool co-ops, furniture co-ops, farm co-ops, book co-ops, arts and crafts co-ops, apartment co-ops.

Your problem is: (1) finding or founding one in your community; and (2) making your dealings with the co-op pleasant.

For No. 1, see the bibliography in this excellent book: *Food Co-ops for Small Groups; How To Buy Better Food for Less*, Tony Vellela, Workman Publishing Co., 1975, $2.95.

For No. 2, keep in mind that strong people have strong opinions, which will inevitably clash with other strong people's opinions. Use the patterning techniques in your meetings together so that the focus is on ideas, not personalities. And remember you don't have to pretend to *like* the people with whom you cooperate. You can be friendly and curious and respectful of the others, but that doesn't automatically make you bosom friends.

In our own life, we've participated in a babysitting co-op, a once-a-week fresh vegetable co-op, a three-family meal exchange three times a week, a housework exchange, a remodeling labor exchange, and a 500-household food co-op (Briarpatch) in which we all exchange labor for greatly lowered prices and greatly heightened sharing. Some of these co-ops were one-time affairs; some we quit when we didn't need them anymore (e.g., babysitting); and some we expect to belong to for years.

When we have a chore or need that we share with others, we consider cooperation first. And you don't have to join an organization for cooperation—some of our most pleasant cooperative efforts have been with old friends.

2. PUBLIC LIBRARIES

We can't hide it: we love libraries. For every hour we spend in one, it feels like we gain four; we're expanded by new ideas, by new insights, by new resources.

When we are considering a major purchase, we go to the library and research it so we won't waste time and money buying a lemon. When we want to see what famous artists have to say and far-away museums hold, we go to the library. When we want to laugh, escape, or be inspired, we go to the humor or detective or adventure or science fiction or biography section of the library. When we want to learn how to fix our car or why our daughter acts differently at seven than six, we go to the library.

When we have questions about anything, we go to the

library, or call one. A good library is an entry into the collected knowledge, experience, and wisdom of the human race.

Librarians are human. Occasionally you will run into a prune who seems to resent sharing books or knowledge, but it's a prune who accidentally happens to be a librarian. Most are sincerely happy to help you. With the prunes, be persistent. And learn the system (Library of Congress or Dewey Decimal) for your library, so you can find material yourself.

Don't forget that the same classifications (with possible prefixes such as ''j'') are used on children's, reference, and oversized books, but these may be hidden away somewhere else in the library. Ask your librarian.

3. ACCESS TO RESOURCES

"You know the one," she said. "That restaurant run by Vietnamese refugees behind the lawyers' building—fantastic food, fantastic prices. You don't know about it? That's because they aren't in the phone book and don't advertise. You just have to *know* about it."

There are a lot of great resources in the world that you have to just *know* about—like *Freebies*, the newsletter of free things (P.O. Box 5605, Santa Monica, CA 90405, $12/5 issues), or *Medical Self-Care* (P.O. Box 717, Inverness, CA 94937, $7/year). These resources won't be advertised on TV, on radio, or in newspapers or magazines; nor will they be found on newsstands or in big bookstores.

Many of these little-known but helpful resources are self-published books or pamphlets. They are written, designed, typed, sent to the printer, distributed, and promoted all by the same person(s). Rarely is that person in it for the money; even more rarely does a self-publisher have much money available for advertising.

And yet these small self-published newsletters, pamphlets, magazines, and books often contain the most honest, helpful, time-and-money-saving advice you'll ever read. So how can you find out about them?

There are some accesses to these resources that you can read and follow regularly. When you read them, be sure to carry a pad and pen to jot down useful titles, names, and addresses: *Co-Evolution Quarterly*, Box 428, Sausalito, CA 94965, $12/year; *The Mother Earth News*, P.O. Box 70, Hendersonville, NC 28739, $12/year; *Mother Jones*, 607 Market St., San Francisco, CA 94105, $12/year.

Your librarian can help you keep informed about other information sources.

4. GETTING UP EARLIER/STAYING UP LATER

If you really want to do something on your own time that requires a stretch of uninterrupted quiet and if you live with others, you may have trouble. Naturally the people around you want to talk and laugh and play with you. A solution is either to get up earlier or stay up after everyone else has gone to bed.

Perhaps you're inclined toward the former, early rising, and yet when that alarm goes off, you can't bear to leave that warm bed? Try doing it in small steps, just as you started other activities on your Wish list. At first get up early once a week and only ten minutes earlier than normal. Be sure to lay out warm clothes near the bed the night before, so you won't freeze, and have the material for whatever you want to do ready: books, art media, paper and pencil, gardening tools, running shoes.

If you come to treasure these quiet hours alone, you may want gradually to get up earlier and earlier. There is a reciprocal need to go to bed earlier, too.

The procedure for staying up later is the same: have your materials ready and ease into the extended hours gradually. It may help fight fatigue to cut down on coffee in the morning so that you can take a short nap on your lunchtime or before dinner. Exercise will also help you stay alert later and even get along on a little less sleep.

5. CHILDREN'S BOOKS

So many of us hamper our natural curiosity by thinking that if we don't know how to do something such as carpentry or drawing by the time we're adults, we've missed our chance forever. This is a needless straitjacket. And yet if you try to conquer these mental blocks by reading an adult how-to book, you may be further frustrated by verbose text, explanations based on other knowledge you don't have, or too much information.

Children's books to the rescue! They are simple, direct, uncomplicated, well-illustrated, and nonthreatening. The next time you want to learn about something that halfway scares you, visit the children's section of your library or a good bookstore.

And don't forget the children's fiction department. Many adults regret ''not having time to read anymore.'' Though it sounds silly, one of the satisfying aspects of reading children's books, besides the superb writing, is that most books can be finished in one or two sessions. Try reading *Charlotte's Web* by E. B. White or *A Wrinkle in Time* by Madeleine L'Engle or *I Am the Cheese* by Robert Cormier. Again, your librarian will help you find books suited to your reading tastes.

6. SOME MACHINES

Although most of our "time-saving" machines in reality gobble up our time, there *are* machines that can help you use and enjoy your time better:

1. An inexpensive wind-up kitchen timer can serve as the alter ego you may need to limit your more foolish uses of time. For example, if you scrub walls that are already clean because you can't decide what else to do, put a definite time limit on housecleaning. Remember Parkinson's Law that work expands to fill the time available and set the timer for fifteen or twenty minutes. Quit cleaning when it rings and do something more satisfying; use the minutes it's ticking away to decide what you prefer to do. You are the only person who can control how much time to spend on the never-ending chores (see Idiot Work under 4. Trivia in Part Three: A Bag of Tricks). The timer can also be used to get a reluctant kid off to school in the morning or to take over your anxiety about leaving the house on time for an appointment.

2. A bicycle offers you so many pleasures: the outdoors, moderate exercise, downright smugness that you can go where cars can't, free parking, and you don't pollute the air. Although it may take more time to travel (and this is

debatable—in cities during rush hours, the bicycle has repeatedly won the commuter race), riding a bike forces you to pause and consider whether the trip is really necessary.

3. Despite all the fuss mentioned in the Time-gobblers section, the telephone can save you hours; call stores to check on hours and prices, check on appointments and engagements, and so forth.

4. The radio has often been a life-enricher and time-saver for us, specifically public radio. We listen to "Newspapers for the Blind," the local newspaper read aloud, while we clean house; we enjoy interviews with inspiring artists while we do handcrafts; we are exposed to a wide variety of music as we remodel. Similar time-saving devices are the tape recorder and the record player, for listening to pleasures such as *Books on Tape* (P.O. Box 71405, Los Angeles, CA 90071 [free catalog], poems and short stories read aloud, and of course music. (Your public library probably lends such tape cassettes and records.)

Choose and use your machines carefully, to make sure they're not gobbling your time, and then enjoy them thoroughly.

7. CHILDREN

Children have a natural need to be loved and to love. Until about the age of six, they show their love by wanting to participate in everything with you. If you give them small tasks to do next to you, according to their age and dexterity, they will be ecstatic.

Before long, with practice, the children can be extremely

helpful in getting family tasks accomplished, just as they did when a greater percentage of us lived on farms than in cities. This help is as time-saving as the old practice of having the neighbors over for a barn raising.

Little by little, with your encouragement, kids can learn to take care of themselves—wash their own bodies and hair, pack their own lunches, wash their clothes, cook, do dishes, clean up their rooms, help around the house.

Not only that, but kids have great ideas. The next time you feel time-frazzled, ask your children what they think you should do to get it all done. Listen with respect and you'll be amazed at the ingenuity of their answers. You'll also laugh a lot, and not always at the kids.

Unfortunately, many parents rob their children of this natural proclivity to help. Even beyond the baby stage, some grown-ups make all decisions for their children—whether they're cold and need a sweater, whether they're hungry or full, whether their room needs cleaning, what classes they should take after school—and they always tell kids they're too inept or too young to help. It's a self-fulfilling prophecy: soon the children lose all interest in helping. Then parents begin complaining about how much time raising the children takes, but by then it's too late.

Your children can and will help, if you let them. And more importantly, they can help you to enjoy life more, by reacquainting you with that forgotten art of playing with no goal but play, one of the keys to living a full and satisfying life.

8. COMMUNITIES

It is hard to feel a part of the modern city, with its frantic activity, anonymity, and bureaucracy. And yet the quality of a city is determined by its citizens. Whether you have a people-oriented community or not depends on how much you've spoken up.

Do you care about the air in your city? The number of parks? The condition and welfare of the entire city, not just the nice parts? City support for the arts, alternate technology, transportation, housing?

Working to make your neighborhood or community a pleasant place to live is worth your time, even though it's not always easy or fast.

Some of the more colorful people-generated community activities we've observed are block parties, where a street is closed off and everybody feasts together; neighborhood associations to clean up, fight crime, and help each other; town meetings and town picnics; community gardens; eccentric festivals like San Francisco's Artist Soap-Box Derby; and anything that makes neighbors smile and feel proud of their community.

9. MAIL-ORDER GUIDES

There is almost nothing you can't buy through the mail now (including stamps). You don't always save money, but by choosing products wisely and by not buying anything you don't need or want, you can stretch your time.

The time you save shopping by mail is great, but it can also enrich your life in other ways. You can, for example, recapture that delicious expectation while wait-

ing for the goods to arrive, that excitement you last felt
when you sent away for your Captain Midnight Secret
Decoder Ring.

There are too many interesting mail-order firms to list
here, but you can find guides for all these categories and
more:

- Food (fruit, meats, cheeses, nuts, seeds, grains,
  specialty imports)
- Gifts (including handmade gifts—see 5. Shopping
  in Part Three: A Bag of Tricks)
- Clothing
- Furniture
- Entertainments (games, books, records, video
  tapes)
- Government property (stamps, surplus bookcases
  and desks, cars)

Watch the ads in your favorite magazines and newspapers and ask the librarian in your public library to help you
find what you want.

One negative side of ordering by mail is that a tidy business has developed of selling your name and address to
every other mail-order firm under the sun. Soon your mail
pile overflows with offers and come-ons and appeals for
what turns out to be garbage. If you wish to stop the ava-
lanche, you may write the following place and ask to have
your name removed from the junk mail lists:

Direct Mail/Marketing Association, Inc.
6 East 43 Street
New York, NY 10017

10. SERENDIPITY

These are some of the small, clever eurekas our friends and students have invented that make life's ragged edges a little smoother. No doubt you know some yourself.

- A woman who had trouble making herself write letters to relatives selected smaller stationery. "I filled three pages fast and felt I'd fulfilled my duty, even though those three tiny pages wouldn't fill one normal one."
- A divorced father does all his cooking for the week on Sunday morning, freezing a week of main dishes. This is not a new idea for many women, but it was absolutely liberating for him.
- A female doctor carries small pregummed labels in her pocket. When she hears or reads about a good book or an event she wants to attend, she writes it on a label. Later she sticks the label on her calendar or in the notebook she carries to the library.
- A retired woman keeps 3 × 5″ index cards in her pocket. She copies inspiring passages on the cards (with a title, author, publisher, date, price, and Dewey Decimal number), puts a key word on the top right, and files the card under various categories in a recipe file box beside her bed. She enjoys sharing these quotes, when appropriate, in letters to her friends, who are scattered around the world.
- Another library freak uses his 5 × 7″ 13-ring business telephone directory, which takes 2½ × 3½″ address slips, to record what books and magazines he want to read. He uses the alphabet dividers that

come with the directory as Dewey Decimal dividers. When he finds and finishes a book, he jots down his opinion of it at the bottom of the slip and files it in the back of the book. From time to time he enjoys rereading his comments on what he's read.

- An artist bought seven clipboards and seven different colored pads of paper. Each color stands for one day of the week. He makes lists of what needs to be done on the appropriate days; all seven clipboards hand neatly on the wall of his studio. Formerly writing all those lists on one white piece of paper was boring and intimidating to him; but the colors cheer him up, so he feels more like doing all the work.

- A woman who was always late with holiday and birthday gifts began giving promises: a beautiful rectangle of card stock listing in calligraphy three choices of handmade gifts. The giftee chooses what he or she wants and in what colors and the woman then sets to work making the gift. She says knowing that the gift is wanted and anticipated brings pleasure and speed to making it.

- A man who does all the grocery shopping since his wife went back to work made a master plan of the aisles in their grocery store. He photocopied the master plan and keeps a copy on the bulletin board beside the refrigerator. As items are needed, she or he writes them on the list under the correct aisle. Then at shopping time, he grabs the list and zips through the store.

- A family tapes a sheet of blank newsprint (available cheap in large rolls from newspapers) to the entire top of the telephone desk. Messages, memos, reminders, doodles, ideas, and gripes soon fill the page. When all has been relayed, acted upon, passed on, reacted to, and sometimes framed, a new sheet replaces the old. (Be sure to leave a set of marking pens in rainbow colors on the desk, too.)

On Dealing with Others:
Five Final Messages

1. Conquer lateness
2. Learn to live as a couple ("She's-an-early-riser-I-prefer-the-nighttime, He's-always-late-I-hate-waiting" blues)
3. Give your time to others
4. Watch your language
5. Respect others' time

1. CONQUER LATENESS

If you are perpetually late, it doesn't matter whether you understand *why* you're late. Knowing that you're late because you're putting off final judgment of yourself and your work does not help you break the habit of being late, but the following might. (NOTE: Early and on-time arrivers, don't read this. You will not, cannot, appreciate its liberating importance to the always-late. In fact, it won't even make sense to you.)

You probably never *intend* to be late. It's just that in calculating how long it takes to get there on time, you underestimate your slop time—delays in traffic, in a slow-starting car, in walking from the bus. After thirty or forty years of this, you have begun to suspect that it's deeper than simple miscalculation. Still, you have to *do* something about it. You may have tried adding 15 minutes to your calculations and still have been late, to your disgust.

Being late has nothing to do with actual time; it is a matter of putting off the deadline (e.g., the exact time of an appointment). As long as you have internalized the *actual* time, are mentally aiming for, say, an 11 AM doctor's appointment, you will undoubtedly be late. The deadline, 11 AM, is what you're putting off. Even adding 15 minutes to your preparation time, you will mysteriously end up arriving later than 11 AM.

Here's the real secret: give yourself permission to move up the deadline. Say to yourself, "I can arrive at the doctor's office at 10:45 AM. Arriving at 10:45 AM is what I'm aiming for. The deadline is 10:45 AM." I'll calculate to be there at 10:45 AM." The time 10:45 goes into your internal clock. You will probably be late, as usual. You will arrive at 10:55 AM, ten minutes late, but technically early for the 11 AM appointment.

To anyone who doesn't know how awful it feels to be perennially late, this sounds idiotic, but it works and it's liberating. Suddenly, you realize you don't have to be late anymore. However, since you are changing a habit ingrained since childhood, you will have to examine one by one and reset each and every deadline you face every day, until being early becomes a new habit for you. You are

supposed to pick up the kids at 5 PM? Plan to be there at
4:45 PM. Your deadline is 4:45 PM. Tennis date at 6 PM?
Be there at 5:45. Meeting at 7:30 PM? You aim to arrive
at 7:10 PM; all your travel calculations are geared to arriving at 7:10 PM. Christmas shopping always done at the last
minute? Aim to be finished at Thanksgiving. Write on your
calendar two weeks before Thanksgiving: "Buy (or make)
Mom's present." Do you always begin packing for vacation at midnight the evening before you leave? Give yourself permission to be packed *three days* before you leave,
even if it means buying extra underwear or whatever so
you'll have something to wear in the interval between when
you're packed and when you leave.

Change your *deadline*, not your slop time. Give yourself
permission to change the deadline. You'll still be secretly
neurotic; you'll still be secretly late because you'll undoubtedly miss your new deadline like you missed the old;
but on the surface, to the world, you'll appear to arrive on
time, perhaps even early. (If this works for you, better
learn to take a book along to read while you wait.)

2. LEARN TO LIVE AS A COUPLE ("SHE'S-AN-EARLY-RISER-I-PREFER-THE-NIGHTTIME, HE'S-ALWAYS-LATE-I-HATE-WAITING" BLUES)

What can you do when your time sense and living rhythms
conflict with your mate's? Can this marriage be saved?
When sex, money, or children seem to be the area of conflict, underneath there often lurks, unspoken, a clash of
time senses.

There are so many variations of time-arrangement and

time-value that you can count on differing from your mate in some way that will cause conflict. Unfortunately, we inherit our time values from our parents and culture, and they are so integral to our personality that we take them totally for granted—until we run into someone with different time values. these basic assumptions are not often examined or expressed. (See Part four: Perspectives.) Instead, we find ourselves arguing with our mate about the cats not being fed, for example, instead of one person admitting he's mad at the other for waiting until the last minute to get dressed and leave for work.

Based on our own struggles to live well together, we offer the following guidelines for couples:

First, each of you, identify your personal patterns. You did this for your activities in Part One: Action, but now reexamine your natural rhythms—highs and lows during the day, month, cycle, year, ten-year period. Don't try to do this for your mate. You can guess at his or her rhythms, but that person is the only one who really knows what *is* for him or her.

Second, talk about what these three usually unarticulated time problem areas mean to you:

A. What, exactly, do you mean when you say "in a little while," "soon," "later," and "a long time from now"? It used to be that when Robbie called home at 4 PM and said, "I'll be home in a little while," Tony expected to see her about 4:45 PM. But Robbie puttered around, finishing this and that, glanced at the clock at 5 PM, and thought, "Well, I better start home." She arrived at 5:30 PM, "in a little while" for her and "late" for Tony. Now Tony doesn't believe her, and things go much more smoothly.

B. What is your late factor? How many minutes after a

specified appointment time can you arrive without feeling angry or upset? Does your mate differ? Tony defines "late" as one minute after the specific time. He hates to wait and he hates to be late (which he interprets as making others wait). Robbie is chronically late, but doesn't care if it's "only" 15 minutes late. Fortunately, she finally discovered the secret of how to be on time (see Conquer Lateness).

We wasted much time hassling each other over lateness, until we brought our unspoken definitions out into the open and agreed to accommodate each other.

C. What are your hot and cold periods, and how do they differ from your mate's? Robbie loves to get up at 5:30 AM to write. Tony wakes up slowly and hates to be chirped at by happy writers before 10 AM. By 9 PM, Robbie has zonked out, especially if we're at the movies, but Tony's body—especially his nudging elbow—is starting to really wake up.

Third, respect your own rhythms; respect your partner's rhythms. There are many ways to go through life. Your way is the best for you, but not for everybody. Prepare to compromise with a song on your lips. It's easier that way.

Finally, keep talking. It is the unspoken assumptions that cause serious problems. They must be aired to be resolved, especially the ones (like time assumptions) that most people rarely think about. but retain your sense of humor while communicating and learn how to fight productively instead of dredging up the same arguments each time. We found helpful *The Intimate Enemy: How To Fight Fair in Love and Marriage*, by Dr. George R. Bach and Peter Wyden (William Morrow & Co., 1969, $8.95, 301.42B). We also like to have nude pillow fights and bash the hell out of each other. We always end up laughing.

3. GIVE YOUR TIME TO OTHERS

There is no greater gift in this Age of Hurry than to give your time to others. It can mean far more to the receiver than a mere package wrapped in colored paper.

Dr. Hans Selye, a pioneer in the studies of the body's reaction to stress, calls giving your time to others "altruistic egoism." You give your time because it feels good and because you're selfish: a lower stress level and greater calmness are your reward.

This kind of giving can be perverted, like everything else in life. But the test for this perversion is easy: do you *expect* gratitude, and are you disappointed when you don't get it? If so, consider pulling back. The world has enough *real* martyrs.

4. WATCH YOUR LANGUAGE

Your attitude is reflected in the language you use. When you say, "There isn't enough time," you imply that outside circumstances control your life, when you are in fact allowing them to control you.

What happens when you change your language? You become an active *chooser* instead of a passive victim. Try it:

Old Language	*New Language*
There isn't enough time.	That's not how I want to spend my time.
I'm too busy.	I don't want to do it.
I don't have time.	I choose to do other things.

5. RESPECT OTHERS' TIME

Now that you've set up ways to accomplish everything you want to get done—ways that often involve eliminating distractions and interruptions—extend to others the same courtesies you expect.

Ask your friends when they prefer to receive telephone calls and when they do not. Write their answers under their names in your phone book. When you call someone say, "Is this a good time to talk? Do you have five minutes?" Then don't go over this limit unless *they* want to.

For appointments and get-togethers, arrive on time and leave on time. An enjoyable dinner together can be ruined by an uncomfortable lingering departure.

Naturally, respecting others' time applies most to your family. Provide for your children and mate what you want for yourself: the freedom to arrange your time so that life is fun, nonhurried, nonfragmented, and satisfying.

Part Four

PERSPECTIVES

It is only in appearance that time is a river.
It is rather a vast landscape and it is the
eye of the beholder that moves.

Thornton Wilder, *The Eighth Day*

Do you think you invented frantic?

You are stumbling toward the bathroom, barefoot, in the middle of the night. You step on a tack. Your whole body short-circuits in a brilliant flash of pain. What do you do next?

Chances are, the last thing you would do is review the latest theory of how pain impulses travel to your nervous system. People just don't operate that way.

No, you howl, and remove the tack from your sole.

When you are upset, anxious, uncomfortable, or in pain, the most urgent thing for you to do is to remove the source of pain or discomfort, to deal with the upset and anxiety. Obvious as this is in the simple case of the embedded tack, we forget this for less clear-cut discomforts. And other people usually don't help.

The most common and least appreciated advice about

pain, discomfort, upset, or anxiety is that you shouldn't feel it—advice usually offered while you are still suffering, and always for reasons which are purely those of the advisor. In terms of tacks in the foot: after your first howls, your spouse says you shouldn't feel the pain, because it's inconvenient to have people in pain in the middle of the night, and besides, it'll wake the children. . . . Others might offer these bits of wisdom:

1. "I *told* you not to leave the tacks where the kids (cat) could knock them on the floor."
2. "Oh, I once stepped on a tack. . . ."
3. "Gosh, yes, everyone hates to step on tacks."
4. "Don't let it bother you . . . only three people have died of tetanus in this state since 1950."
5. "Shut up! I'm trying to get some sleep!"

No one needs to tell you to pull the tack out. . . .

In the case of the tack, it's easy to see the utter uselessness of any advice that doesn't deal directly with your first urgent reaction—to alleviate the pain. Your reaction to such useless advice is outrage.

Concern with the way you use your time is, first of all, a discomfort. You don't even think about managing your time unless you're bothered by the way you use time now. When you moan in anguish, "I can't get it all done!" the standard reactions of others are not that different from those listed above for tack-in-foot:

1. "Well, you shouldn't have told them you'd take care of it." (The "I-told-you-so" reaction.)
2. "I had a day like that last week." (Irrelevant personal history.)

3. "Who can? That's how it is these days." (It's a common problem, so it doesn't exist.)

4. "You think that's bad. You should have two jobs like me." (It could be worse.)

5. "That's nice. Excuse me, I have to go to my meeting." (That's your problem. Don't bother me.)

The approach that we've deliberately taken in this book (in Part One: Action) is, "Well, what do you have to do? Good. Now do *something* to remove the pain. And get on with it."

Lest we bludgeon the tack metaphor to death, we will only point out two more things.

First, after you pull the tack out, you continue on to the bathroom, your original intention. In the same way, the whole point of personal time management is to remove the pain and *get on with living*.

Second, if you are at all reasonable and if the pain has sufficiently impressed you, you will give a little thought to avoiding a repetition. Two simple solutions will leap into your mind: control the tacks, and protect your feet. Both are perfectly reasonable ideas, until you consider how unpredictable kids or cats actually are, and thus how uncontrollable, or when you consider the inappropriateness of putting on your hiking boots in the middle of the night just to hit the john. No, a moment's reflection, and you see that neither the tacks nor unshod feet are what really brought you such pain.

Actually it was because *you were walking in the dark*.

A little light, please

Part One: Action helps you remove the pain; the tricks are there to keep new pain away. Now to cast some light on the basic problems.

What follows is an examination of how we unconsciously perceive time, what unuttered premises we have about time, and how our feelings about use of time can cause us great distress. All this is offered for relief of pain. Understanding what's behind the clock face can aid and comfort you for a variety of reasons:

1. Knowing that the pain is common makes you feel less like a freak . . . and it *is* common. Or did you think you invented Frantic?
2. Stating the unspoken, bringing it out in the open, has the salutary effect of giving us a starting point for solving time problems.
3. Many of the observations reported here have until now been scholarly or academic. It's time to apply them, practically, to our lives.

Remember, in all that follows, the ideas are presented to help you relieve your pain.

Images of Time

If you were to ask the average American to explain his concept of time, you would probably first get a blank stare. "After all, time is such a simple idea; and your concept of time is probably the same as mine, right? And besides, what do you mean?"

Maybe it would be better to ask for a picture. And the picture you would get would fall into one of two categories. The first would be a clock face (kids usually do this, confusing the measuring device with what is measured). After that, the most common picture would be a line. And all refinements would be one form or another of this line.

One common variation is the arrow,

which adds direction, a representation of movement from past to future.

Asked to refine further this image of time, most people will be quick to add a division or segmentation into units.

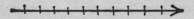

Variations of this picture are the road:

and sometimes a wavy, ribbonlike strip, or river.

Common to all these images of time are three qualities. It is conceived of as being:

1. Linear (one-dimensional only [even in the last two pictures, which have a two-dimensional appearance, the important idea is one-dimensional]).
2. Segmented (broken up into intervals or compartments).
3. Directional (with the future direction of far more importance to us than the past [and the future is something we feel has to be controlled by planning and scheduling]).

This rather simple picture of the concept "time," which most people never confront consciously, brings with it some problems. Before we examine them, it should be noted that after the exercise of sketching out one's notion of time, most people ask, "Is there any *other* way to look at it?" The question itself points out that this view, at least among Americans, is ingrown, unconscious, unexamined, and considered "natural" in some sense. Can you imagine some other way of picturing time?

The linear, segmented, future-oriented image of time, as "natural" or God-ordained as it may seem to us, is by no means the only one. It is, in fact, a minority view on our planet, one which has come about through a complex series of cultural, technological, philosophical—and yes—religious causes. Only Americans, Germans, and Swiss share this time view in its pristine form. Let us briefly mention other possibilities before pressing on to the consequences of our time image.

Note, first, that we always have to use some kind of spatial metaphor to describe time, and the descriptions below are all of this type. Indeed, we do this constantly in our language: events are a "long" time or "short" time ago, it happened "around the same time" and so on. This need for spatial imagery hints again that "time" is no simple concept.

Another "natural" image of time is that of a circle, deriving from the cyclic nature of many observable phenomena: the day-night cycle, the crop cycles, the seasons and the tides. Some of the earliest measuring devices—the circle of stones at Stonehenge, sun clocks, sundials—physically used this image. In fact, our clocks until the past decade or so have been round-faced. (The digital watch is a late departure from this and has been adver-

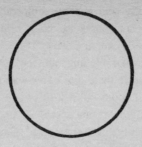

tised as a more "modern" way of telling time. Switching from dials to digital counters seems to be the latest version of progress).

It is also possible to have no concept of time as measurable, as the Eskimos did before exposure to Europeans. For these, the present is a point at which we stand and there is no measuring of time—only synchronization with the sea's tides. Cross-cultural studies of what we call primitive peoples show many subtle variations of the lack of measurable time. In fact, some languages have no separate word for "time."

Another possibility for a time image is to consider it a plane (two-dimensional) or a space or field (three-dimensional imagery), extending in many directions, and yet another is to imagine it as one eternal Now (the mystic's view that all times are one time).

So there *are* other concepts of time, hard as it is for us to imagine them and unnatural as they may seem to us. Our minority view of time is, in fact, incomprehensible to most of the citizens of the earth and one of the sources of our noncommunication with other cultures. "Time" is a very high-level abstraction, instead of the simple concept we usually think it is. Famous child psychologist Piaget claims that it takes a child a dozen years to understand fully and use our culturally conditioned view of time.

THE THREE ASPECTS OF OUR PICTURE OF TIME

Our linear, segmented, future-oriented notion of time affects what we do and how we feel about it.

Because we view time as *linear*, we think it is necessary to sequence all our activities in time. We feel that this in only as it should be and that there is no other way of doing it. Putting cart before horse, we forget that time *seems* linear because we are in the habit of sequencing activities.

Sequencing generates a way of using time which the anthropologist Edward J. Hall calls "monochronic." The preferred way of doing things in the monochronic culture is "one thing at a time," and one who cannot arrange his activities this way is looked at askance and even thought of as sloppy or disorganized.

People of certain other cultures, in which it is natural to be doing a variety of things all at once, seem inefficient, ludicrous, or stupid to us, when in fact they are only using time according to their image of it—"polychronically" or allowing many activities at once. To these same people we appear hurried to the point of madness.

Two questions arise:

1. Is it *bad* to be polychronic or monochronic? As a moral question, this is not as ridiculous as it sounds, and later we shall deal with it.
2. Is there any other way to be?

Perhaps the only reasonable answers are (1) only if it bothers you, and (2) yes and no. In America today, it is difficult to be a polychronic person, if only because the whole culture is so overwhelmingly monochronic. Some of the most frazzled, harried people are those who are forced by their situations to be polychronic, to handle too many things at once. The mother of small children in a monochronic culture like America is an obvious example.

Segmentation, the second characteristic, complements our linear view of time. Time can be chopped up into segments. Time can thus be perceived as a thing, something solid, something that can be, following our American mercantile bent, treated as a commodity. Our language reflects this. We waste time, make time, fill time, buy time, give time, take time, manage time. Time is money.

Some results of our use of time-language are: we feel compelled to use time; that is, we can't just let if flow over us, pass us by. Very few of us pass time, as is linguistically the case in other cultures. We are very active, extremely antsy people. If it is possible for us to fill out time, like a container, then we can ask how densely our time can be filled, how many activities we can pack into a container (month, week, hour) of time. How efficiently can we stuff our day? And in fact, we do this even in our personal lives, adding to the idea of efficient packing a moral dimension that seems, bluntly, insane to those not raised in our culture. ("Idle hands are the devil's helpmates.") We, of course, reciprocate by treating people of other cultures as if they are less advanced versions of ourselves, people who haven't yet discovered the beauty of a high-speed efficient, moral modern life.

And last, the *future orientation* of America is legendary. Our notion of progress, our mania for planning and controlling everything, and our obvious pride in all of this are well-known throughout the world.

The one thing we can say about the results of this linear, segmented, future-oriented time view is this: it works. The material successes these attitudes (and our methods for implementing these attitudes) have brought us are at the same time admired, envied, and hated by other nations.

But we must qualify: it works on the level of material welfare. It worked in getting us to our high standard of living. When we examine the emotional state of much of America, however, there's a question of whether it works at all. Let's look at the negative side of it.

The *linearity*, the "one-thing-at-a-time" aspect of our time view, gets things done for us; it can also lead to tunnel vision and rigidity.

Our *segmentation* of time, and its related notions of efficiency and productivity, so dominant in our work time, can spill over into our nonwork lives. The result can be a feeling of fragmentation, a sense of life as unconnected actions: the "I've-got-to-get-it-together" feeling. The compulsion to fit more and more activities (still sequenced, of course) into less and less time results in what has been called "hurry sickness," and we all seem to have a touch of that at times.

The *future orientation*, with its related enthusiasm for planning and controlling all activities, can also schedule out of our lives the satisfactions we need to enjoy ourselves, at the same time that it ensures the fulfillment of our high-priority productive goals. We succeed at scheduling time and fail at living a full, satisfying, nonharried life.

The Work/Free Time Split

There is another side to our view of time which causes us pain more insidiously than those discussed above. Once again, it is necessary to state explicitly something so taken for granted that we are functionally unaware of it. In America, and in other lands influenced by Western European culture, we all live by an artificial division of time even stronger than the night/day dichotomy:

Work Time/Free Time

What "work" time is, all of us but the idle or independently wealthy surely understand. And "free" time, of course, is nothing other than the time left over after work time. So much for simplicity; so much for intuitive definitions, and what we all take for granted: the common wisdom takes us only this far.

We live as if they're two lives that don't touch and as if you can have one in order but not the other. Like the mind/body split, this is a useful abstract distinction, but in no sense real.

Looking one level deeper, we find that we really don't have a basic understanding of this work/free split, that we are actually deluding ourselves. Let's check out "work" time first.

Of all the self-evident aspects of work time, it is least arguable that we all consider work time as time which is *not our own*. It is time over which we have no control, or at least we must actively struggle to control it, to direct it toward our personal goals.

For example, suppose that you work for someone else—most people in America do. Most likely you have definite hours to work (and the mere mention of this fact had undoubtedly caused your heartbeat to pick up somewhat). You cannot be late for work—consistently, and for more than a few minutes each time—without drawing down on yourself the wrath of your employer, your immediate supervisor and, if the lateness is sufficiently noticeable, of the more disgruntled workers around you. It's not a question at all of whether this reaction to your lateness is appropriate, rational, or (in the case of the last group mentioned) even someone else's proper concern.

The fact is, all the people involved feel strongly that you are cheating by using for your own individual purposes a commodity which is not yours to use—time—which belongs to someone else, company time. The usual attitude toward habitual latecomers at work supports it; as a rule, they are held in the same easy contempt as petty thieves. The same holds true for leaving early, whether or not there is work to be done, for long lunch hours, coffee breaks, and any other such infringements on company time.

The above, of course, is a description only of the more socially esteemed white-collar job. Should you be locked into a punch-the-clock position, your observance of company time has to be even more strict, or you can start applying for unemployment.

As an exercise, rate the status of a person's position in any company by the discretion he has in arranging his own time. A rough rule of thumb is this: the less control of his work time a person has, the more his work time is in the control of others, the lower his status. The secretary who waits on her boss's every whim, who uses all her time ministering to him, generally has low status in the eyes of the group. The planner, regardless of job title, who can make his own hours, is envied by almost all others. The manager, who not only controls the use of his own time but that of others, is the object of fear as well an envy.

While it may seem that a person of higher status—someone who apparently controls the work time of others and has more discretion in the use of his own—should be freer of the prison of work time, this is not the case. The alarming proliferation in the past thirty years of the men who are obsessed with their jobs clearly shows this. The term "workaholic," coined as late as 1970 (see *Confessions of a Workaholic*), struck such a responsive chord, described the situation so well, that it has become a standard term in the work environment.

What is a workaholic? A person—usually male, though not always—whose addiction to work becomes unbearable to himself and others near him. In terms of our work/free breakdown, he is a person who had so confused himself that he progressively shifts more and more of his free time over to work time, so that he approaches the limit of allowing himself no free time at all. Such workaholics rarely use time efficiently. The compulsion is rather to devote more and more *time*, not accomplishment, to work ("Can't get anywhere in this business unless you put in extra hours"—not extra *work*).

A compelling study of this phenomenon, which gave it the name "Lockheed syndrome" (1971), enumerated the sufferings its victims undergo. Among them are insomnia, anxiety, high stress reactions, ulcers and other diseases, family problems, alcoholism, divorce, and a high percentage of nervous breakdowns.

And yet on the surface, don't we envy and praise this typical sufferer? Aren't hard workers held up for our admiration?

If you are looking for personal satisfaction, you're unlikely to get it during work time. The notable exceptions are those who completely give over their lives to their work and are happy. These are few (and too often those around them suffer a good deal).

It is in our free time, then, that we can try for happiness. But once again, looking under the surface, we find that we have not quite so much of it as we might wish to believe. Most of our free time is not "free." In a day when pundits and social prophets worry about what we will do with all the coming leisure time, it's ironic how little of our new free time can actually be devoted to leisure.

First, out of the 16¼ hours which technically are not work time, about eight must go toward sleep. Some of us need more than eight hours, many of us less; but that leaves the "free" pool at about eight hours. How much of that is "free"?

It takes time to maintain your own body—to feed it,

wash it, groom it; it takes time to maintain your family, especially if there are younger children in it; it takes time to maintain a home (cleaning, laundering, repairing, building, trimming); it takes time not much different from "work" time to do all of these things. It takes times to shop for time-saving devices; it takes time to use them; it takes time to maintain them; and in an ironic shift, it takes time to "enjoy" them. All of these are forms of pseudo-work.

We have been looking at those aspects of our "free" time which take on at least the emotional coloring of work time, those activities which in our free time we cannot seem to avoid. For many of us in America, when we subtract pseudowork time from our "free" time, there is no time left whatsoever. Every activity, every day-filling act, carries with it compulsion, obligation, morality, necessity. For the wife or female counterpart of the workaholic man, for example, even social obligations are a form of work (I'm bringing home the boss for supper. Make sure that we impress the Smythes at the dinner. I've got a deal I'm cooking up for him. . . .").

Though it is currently unfashionable to use the term "housewife," and more than 50 percent of married women now work away from the home in addition to working at home, the housewife holds a special place in the wonderful world of pseudowork time. Note that all of a housewife's time is *technically* "free" time (she doesn't go to the office or plant). The housewife who is exhausted by the end of the day, when hubby gets home and wants attention and service (without reciprocating by giving his attention to her), is so common as to be a comic-strip cliché (Blondie of the Bumsteads).

And the woman who works outside the home is still

expected to manage or maintain the home and to take pride in it. Is it any wonder that there are so many resentful, harried pseudoworkaholic women in America?

There isn't enough time to get it all done in our "free" time, so we begin relinquishing to others, buying time-saving devices and services. Which of the many activities that fill a day do we choose to farm out, and is it worth it? Do we thereby gain a saner, calmer life?

WHAT WE DON'T HAVE TIME FOR

Agreed, we can't expect to get much personal satisfaction during work time. Agreed, we tend to turn our free time into something very much like work time, for reasons we barely understand. Since there is only a limited amount of time available, what *don't* we have time for?

In fact, an enumeration of the documented effects on our lives of our common American lack of time sounds exactly like the ranting of some puritanical moralist: the things we no longer make time for are the things that make life worthwhile, and "saving" time by sidestepping or not doing these things is like tossing the baby out with the dirty bath water.

1. Maintaining our bodies
2. Maintaining and enjoying our possessions
3. Making decisions
4. Enjoying our families
5. Enjoying ourselves—even making love

1. Body Maintenance

There has been a thirty-year trend away from maintaining our bodies. Why? It takes time to do it, time which we're less willing to spend. So, instead of taking the time to bathe, we spend billions on cosmetic coverups: deodorants, which are really perfumes used to hide body odors; toothpastes, which hide bad breath rather than clean teeth; clothes which hide the flab; sprays, which make our hair *look* clean without cleaning it; in short, any number of products which hide the fact that we no longer take the time to take care of our bodies.

Yes, there is a Body Boom, a return in some sense to taking actual care of the body through exercise. But the main reason given for not joining it is still "I don't have the time to run twenty minutes a day." And it is no accident that the "aerobics" approach which began the Body Boom in the late 1960s turned exercise into a form of measurable work and let you rate your productivity by counting points. Something in the American character seems to require countable units.

We don't clean and exercise our bodies because of "no time," and we don't take the time to check what we put into them, either. More and more of the food we eat is either "fast-food" or convenience food from the supermarket. We buy over 40 percent of our food on impulse, strolling down the aisle of a supermarket, snatching whatever catches our eye, a habit well-known and profitable to the sellers. Often the food we thus buy is the most immediately pleasant and the least healthy for us—breakfast cereals which are 75 percent sugar, frozen and fried foods, and so forth. One of the most ironic facts about not taking the time to eat properly is that we are the fattest nation on earth; and despite the arguable claims that we have the best medical care on earth, we are one of the most unhealthy, if we go by the amount of medicines we ingest. The favorite indoor sport of America for the past 25 years has been crash-dieting; the American-made animated feature movie *Hugo the Hippo* recently defined the major difference between animals and humans as, "animals don't take medicine" (a very strange statement, if you think about it).

So we don't take the time to take care of ourselves, and we cover up the resultant mess in fairly superficial cosmetic ways.

2. *Our Possessions: How They Possess Us, And How They Rot Away*

If we don't take time to take care of ourselves, we certainly don' have time to take care of our material goods, much less to enjoy them.

Looking around our homes, we can divide our possessions up into (1) the utilitarian devices and furniture, and (2) our toys. The toys are the possessions we buy mainly for enjoyment, the utilitarian devices for largely productive purposes (often because they are "time-saving").

Do we take care of the Things we own? Hardly. We don't have the time.

American industry doesn't have to plan obsolescence into what it produces, though it does. We are conditioned to use things once or twice, then heave them, or at least put them away to collect dust. And once again, it is only natural that we treat our Things this way. It's simple mathematics: we have so many Things to occupy our attention that the amount of time we have for using and enjoying any specific Thing is extremely small. We are like children

in a nursery overflowing with toys: we move fitfully from
one to another, without the will or ability to stop and enjoy
any one.

Throughout the world Americans, where they are toler-
ated at all, are considered children who are fascinated with
gadgets. And gadget-consciousness is one of the primary
aims of all forms of advertising and sales. Gadgets occupy
a central point in our commercial life. They are almost
exclusively the subject of Christmas gifts, and Christmas
shopping accounts for a good percentage of all nonstaple
goods sold in America. But more importantly, they drain
our time. Consider the emotional envelope of a gadget in
America. It is presented as something irresistibly desirable;
you *have* to have it. As a matter of fact, it couldn't be a
gadget if it were a necessity, but one doesn't take the time
to decide these things; that automatic coffee maker, that
digital watch, that TV computer game is something you
have to have. You buy it, for yourself or for someone else.
And now the true gadget-nature manifests itself; you use it
once, and forever after, whenever you notice it at the back
of the closet or garage, you feel a pang of guilt because
you aren't using it. You may even use it once or twice
more when you don't feel like using it, just because you
have it. You can't enjoy it wholeheartedly, but you can't
bear to keep looking at it. The great new American custom
of the garage sale is the result.

What holds for the pure case of the utterly unnecessary
gadget also holds more or less in the case of our "necessary" possessions. Because we have so many of these
Things, we can't use them all; yet we feel compelled to
use them ("What's the good of owning a lawn mower if
you don't use it?"). The mere fact of owning dictates our

actions, and the more we own, the less time we feel we can devote to using specific goods.

And do we take care of the things we own? Don't be silly! It takes time to take care of your car. Send it to the garage. It takes time to take care of the furnace; send out for the furnace man. It takes time to do almost anything, so we delegate the task to the specialist, who does a terrible job of it and so we have to complain, and so on and so on. The more Things we own, the more likely it is that we'll have the money to pay others to take care of these Things, and the less likely that we'll be able to enjoy the Things. There can be nothing more pathetic than the alienated person for whom all care of Things and family (home, children, spouse, car) has been removed—in other words, for whom all ordinary time-consuming activities are handled by someone else and whose overwhelming response to this is that he or she has no time for anything, as if merely owning something takes time, whether you use it or not.

The anthropologists and economists tell us repeatedly that the higher the standard of living—the more material goods and services generally available—in a culture, the more that member of that culture feels a lack of time.

3. Making Decisions

It takes time to make a decision. Obviously, the actual decision takes place in a second or so. But making a rational decision, one that involves a reasonable choice among understood alternatives, takes the time to gather information, the time to compare alternatives, and the time to consider related information.

As we have seen already, we are taking less and less time to make decisions about shopping for foods and other goods. A possibly rational decision about food shopping would go like this: Plan menus for two weeks. Suppose you plan to have tuna fish salad. When you are shopping, if there are two or more brands of tuna available, compare prices: 9 oz. for 68¢ or 13 oz. for 99¢. Buy whichever satisfies your recipe (otherwise you'll waste some) and whichever is the best buy.

Tuna fish decisions take time. Shrewd food producers and supermarket managers know well that not one in a hundred shoppers will take that time. Half of all female shoppers will take that time. Half of all female shoppers do not even look at the prices, much less compare them, and most money-conscious wives would not dream of letting their husbands loose in the supermarket (some studies have shown that when the man shops, his impulse buying pumps the average checkout bill to over 150 percent of the woman's average bill). The supermarket manager who wants to make a killing in tuna fish takes advantage of our reluctance to use time in decision-making in several simple ways: he displays only one brand of tuna at an insanely high price; shows brightly colored labels preferably with adorable cartoons on them; displays no prices whatsoever; or piles tuna fish cans into a big sales display—8 oz. for 91¢ rather than 9 oz. for 68¢.

But is it worth our while to make rational decisions? Moralizing aside, we can consider the question, if we have so many decisions to make each day, how can we spend enough time to make the right decision? And the higher our standard of living, the more complex our lives seem to be and the more decisions we need to make. And the more decisions needed, the less time we can devote to making each one rationally. Result: the more complicated our lives, the more irrational we are.

It is this state of affairs we refer to when we say, "I've had the craziest day." We are aware that many, if not most, of the decisions we have made were totally arbitrary.

Going back to shopping, in many cases it makes little sense to shop "logically." All of us know someone who carries comparison shopping to such an extreme that he will drive to another city to take advantage of an advertised special, with a savings less than that of the price of gas he uses and a waste of much time.

Obviously it isn't just in shopping that we need to take the time to make decisions. Active, intelligent people like ourselves make choices constantly, and many of them would be better choices if we had time to consider them.

4. The Family Hour

The number of father-strangers if growing. These are the men who may or may not be workaholics, but who have little contact with their children and often with their wives as well. The father who hardly knows his children is a modern folk figure, complete with traditional lines: "I can hardly wait until my kids grow up so I can talk to them." Now the mother who farms out her children is becoming equally noticeable.

Once again, there is another perversion of the "time is money" philosophy into "money is time." Parents who don't have the time for their children often buy that time, either by paying others to keep them or, more directly, by giving the child expensive toys or large allowances. Perhaps as a result of guilt feelings—in America it is culturally unacceptable to ignore your children completely—children are receiving more attention of this kind, and less personal attention from parents than ever before.

Let's not moralize about this; in some families it would even seem beneficial for a child to spend a minimum amount of time in contact with his or her parents. But the cost in terms of frustration seems to be high. The biggest complaint among parental complainers is something like this: "I don't know where he gets those ideas," or its alternate, "I was never like that when I was her age." These are statements of what the 60s called the "Generation Gap," and even discounting the cant which goes with them—the disclaimer of responsibility for embarrassing offspring actions—they are real enough. One of the most undeniable results of recent studies in primate behavior is that most of the socializing behavior of offspring, beyond that small amount programmed by instinct, is learned from parents. No generation of human parents before ours has ever thought of denying that the same is true of human children. Even beyond the fact that the world is different today for our children (for one thing, we didn't have us for parents), it is most unreasonable to expect that the child who sees his parents only during TV station breaks will pattern himself or herself after the parents. And there is support for this idea in the growing number of young people who seem to speak only in sound effects and commercial jingles.

This is all a result of "not having time."

5. Men and Women

We don't have time for love. We hardly have time for sex. Hold it! Isn't America oversexed? Aren't our children experimenting more and at an earlier age? Isn't sex as a whole becoming more casual—home plate on the first date? Isn't pornography, soft and hard-core, approaching pandemic proportions? And what about advertising, entertainment, and women's magazines, which seem sometimes to center exclusively on sex? Isn't that evidence of more time devoted to sex rather than the opposite?

Well, yes, maybe we spend more time thinking about it, talking about it, even looking at various "sanitized" versions of it on TV, but the fact is, we are spending less time doing it. Young couples spend less time getting acquainted before leaping into bed together, but isn't this just another symptom of Hurry Sickness, kids rushing into adult experiences? And while we are preoccupied with sex enough to chuckle nervously at the informal definition of sex as "what we're thinking about when we're not thinking about anything in particular," there is truly no indication that there is any more sex going on than ever before.

When we cut corners in lovemaking, we find trouble: the long-standing woman's complaint that the man never gives her enough time to become aroused; the increasing number of young marrieds who wake from their initial delirium to find themselves staring across the breakfast table at strangers; the conservative estimate that over 50 percent of all married couples suffer some form of sexual dysfunction (impotence, frigidity, premature ejaculation). And the divorce rate is still growing.

Taking pleasure in lovemaking beyond the release of biological tensions takes time. It takes time to get to know a person, as opposed to picking up someone whose function you view as being a carrier of the appropriate complementary genitalia. It takes time, as all the now-necessary love manuals tell us and all the old poets have always told us, to build up the little pleasures and tensions which add joy to what is otherwise an instinct-satisfying pleasure. It takes time to decide whether it is possible to live in close proximity with someone, and fewer people seem to be taking that time.

If you have difficulty believing that less time if being devoted to sex, we can supply some negative evidence. Nine months after the spectacular power outages of the 60s, the hospitals in the blackout areas experienced a dramatic run on the maternity ward. What were these new parents doing before the lights went out?

It really isn't time which is causing all these problems. In some cases the causes are so interwoven and complex that we can't separate them; and certainly in all cases mentioned above, there is no simple cause to be found. Perhaps the only common thread is that we *experience* these complications as part of not having time. "I can't seem to find the time for . . ." (the kids, cleaning house, reading—you fill in the blank).

The most likely cause for our feeling of *no time*, as S.B. Linder has argued so persuasively in *The Harried Leisure Class*, is our affluence. Because we have so many good Things, we have to spend time maintaining, acquiring, consuming, using, and enjoying them. Our relations with other people become more complex, driving us to synchronize and schedule more and more of our activities. But the more activities and goods available, the less time for enjoyment and satisfaction of any particular good or activity. The only escape from this seems to be the vacation, the aim of which is to disengage from all the goods and activities by removing oneself to a simpler environment like a ranch, a seashore, or the mountains. Here, while roughing it (that is, with less Things around), we can recuperate from the accumulated poisons of our regular time, both sexes leaving work and home behind for sanity's sake.

IN SUMMARY

We have lightly explored the major American time breakdown—the work/free time split—and observed that our free
time, while technically increasing, is in fact decreasing.
We live in a time famine. Among the active middle class,
there is a sense of time rushing by; we feel frazzled, hectic,
harried.

We don't have time, and it's not all subjective. Part of
it comes form having too many Things to deal with, and it
pains us.

The painful effect of not having enough time for these
important things is threefold: (1) We do not get the pleasure we expect and require; the result is chronic frustration,
a lack of (or a souring of) our satisfaction. (2) We are
violating a cultural imperative. In our culture, a person
should spend sufficient time on children, family, sex, food,
self-improvement, upkeep of homes and possessions; the
reality (we don't have time for it) pales before the *should*,
and guilty feelings result. (3) The conviction that we aren't
spending the US Recommended Daily Allotment of time
(that we ought to be) on these activities makes us even
more resolved to compress more into less time, escalating
us into yet more harriedness, and we get increasingly frantic.

We thus become more frustrated, feel more guilt, and
get more frantic.

We've inherited a linear, segmented, furture-oriented
image of "time," as well as a work time/free time split.
Work time we make the best of, endure, or surrender to;
it is generally not our own to do with as we please, and
we are under compulsion to be productive for someone else
in our work time. Our free time is what's left over, but

every day we're pressed from another side to turn our free time into pseudowork time.

The "efficiency" methods used to run a business may work for business, but they fail miserably when used to eke satisfaction out of personal life. Applying such principles as "time is money" to your home life wreaks havoc. Unhappiness, dissatisfaction, feelings of being frazzled and harried and of never accomplishing anything worthwhile— all these are the result.

Stop the World!

Is it hopeless? Are you doomed to feel frazzled the rest of your life? No. Quite simply, no. You can change. We've structured the Part One: Action portion of this book to help you direct your own changes.

1. Patterning is a technique based on lateral, not vertical or linear, thinking. You *naturally* think in patterns. Your Life pattern helps you avoid thinking in terms of narrow time slots.
2. The Upper/Downer and Wish lists emphasize activities and their satisfaction, not the scheduling of these activities.
3. Aiming for satisfaction will enable you to ballast unsatisfying activities. Try to keep ticking off satisfactions, not a soulless list of completed tasks.
4. The Presumé helps you track your dreams, which are more important to you than your goals.

You can't easily change the culture around you, but you can change your own use of and feelings about time. Watch out for tacks; protect your feet; remove any pain immediately; and turn on the light.

Another Way

There *are* people in the world who have absolutely no problems with managing their time. They seem to float along, rather unhurried, rarely upset, getting done just about everything they want, and try as you might, you never see them popping tranquilizers or hitting the bottle behind the dieffenbachia.

For these people, much of the preceding discussion is academic. They just aren't uncomfortable enough about their use of time to think it's worth discussing. For the modern *busy* person, these freaks of nature are both an object of envy and an invitation to mayhem.

We asked such a person what rules, if any, he followed. Irritatingly enough, he had none. So we asked him to describe the way he attacked life.

13 Relaxed Ways to Manage Your Time

1. Break it up—then start only what you can finish.
2. Do the *least* you can.
3. Ask yourself, "*Who* says I have to do this?"
4. Ask yourself, "Why do I have to do this *now*?"
5. Wear a watch without a second hand, if you need a watch at all.
6. Learn to say "Yes!" to insistent people, but be insincere.
7. Ask yourself, "Who says *I* have to do this?" (Law of Shirking).
8. Tell yourself, "Ten years from now, this will seem very unimportant" (Law of Perspective).
9. If you absolutely have to do something, set aside some time for doing it when you don't need to eat or sleep.
10. Try *hard* not to worry about getting things done.
11. Only buy T-shirts with pockets (otherwise you're always looking for a place to put things).
12. Don't live by slogans; thinking is better.
13. Don't think in categories; don't go by numbers.

One-Week Calendar

(see pages 200-201)

Enter here what you do or want to do consistently every week. In addition to listing such things as routine cleaning and maintenance chores and children's lessons, we suggest you enter what's on your Wish list and in your Presumé. Make time for your dreams to come true (e.g., write in when you plan to run, to study French, to read a challenging book, to garden, to write letters, play the guitar, visit the library, stare into space). If you own this book, tear out the calendar and post it in a conspicuous place.

One-Year Calendar

(see pages 204-205)

We all have different ideas about what needs to be done regularly throughout the year and how often to repeat a task. You might lube your car twice as often as we do, for example. So the following is only a suggested checklist; add or delete until the list meshes with your wishes. Then enter the task or activity on the One-year Calendar. If you own this book, tear out the calendar and post it where you'll see it from time to time.

ONE-WEEK CALENDAR

	Monday	Tuesday	Wednesday
A.M.			
P.M.			

Thursday	Friday	Saturday	Sunday

MAINTENANCE

Shelter

Outside:

wash windows
check roof and gutters
repair leaks and other nuisances
plant/prune/clean up garden
water/turn/spread compost heap
clean garage

Inside:

shampoo rugs/wash and wax floors
spring and fall housecleaning
clean winter clothes/drapes
turn mattresses
wash windows
clean out fireplace
repair paint chips, moldy windows, etc.

Body (For All Members of Family)

physical checkup (including eyes)
dental checkup
breast examination
cosmetics (haircuts, facials, etc.)
vacations and other irrationalities (see text)
aerobic activities (running, bicycling, swimming, jumping
    rope)
clothing (school, Halloween, party, vacation, etc.)

Transportation

Car, Moped, or Motorcycle:

change oil
lube job
points and plugs
battery
tune-up
tires
vacuum and/or wash

Bicycle:

check condition of tires, tubes, spokes
clean all moving parts (chain, freewheel, chainrings,
    spokes, wheels, etc.)
oil chain and gear pulleys, wheels
repair gear and brake cables

IMPORTANT DATES

Personal

birthdays (family and friends: list names and dates on piece
    of scratch paper to be sure you don't forget anybody and
    file in back of book; enter dates on calendar in two
    places, once on the date and once several weeks before
    as a reminder)
anniversaries

ONE-YEAR CALENDAR

(Some holidays move around from year to year—these are for 1979.)

WEEK	January	February	March	April	May	June
1	New Year's Day	Groundhog Day		April Fools' Day		
2		Lincoln's Birthday / Valentine's Day	Purim	Passover / Palm Sunday	Mother's Day	Flag Day
3	Martin Luther King Day	Washington's Birthday	St. Patrick's Day	IRS and state taxes / Easter		Father's Day
4		Ash Wednesday	vernal equinox			summer solstice
5				Daylight Savings Time begins	Memorial Day	

SALE ITEMS (January): Christmas cards, winter clothing, underwear and lingerie, white goods (linens, towels), relentions and radios, cars, floor coverings, toys—in short, a great month to buy everything you need for a year

SALE ITEMS (March): china, glassware, housewares

SALE ITEMS (May): spring clothing

July	August	September	October	November	December
Independence Day		Labor Day	Yom Kippur	Election Day	
			Columbus Day	Veterans Day	
		autumnal equinox			Hanukkah
		Rosh Hashanah		Thanksgiving	winter solstice / Christmas
			Daylight Savings Time ends / Halloween		New Year's Eve

SALE ITEMS: bathing suits, summer clothing, luggage

SALE ITEMS: furniture, underwear and lingerie, white goods, lawn mowers, major appliances

SALE ITEMS: cars and tires

SALE ITEMS: fall clothing, boots, camping equipment, lawn furniture

SALE ITEMS: houses

holidays, festivals, celebrations (when giving handmade gifts, start months in advance)

six-month Presumé

performances, speeches, museum shows, etc.

Financial

taxes (federal, state, county, and city)

insurance payments (health, life, car, etc.)

monthly payments (car, house, etc.)

savings (no one else will save for you; if you find it hard to do, plan regular deposits by writing dates on calendar)

subscriptions, membership dues, donations

COMMUNITY SERVICE

blood donations

volunteer service

esprit de corps (block parties, neighborhood bands, parades, etc.)

NOTE: Sales tend to come in regular cycles. You can save time and money by knowing the cycle. Objects normally on sale during certain months of the year are entered on the One-Year Calendar.

Tools of Organization

In order to get it all done, you must have an external support system; the absolute minimum is a system for storing, organizing, and generally controlling the Things that will otherwise use up your already scarce time. Not only do you need paper to write your ideas on, but also places to post or file those ideas, places to store the rest of the scrap paper, bookcases for this book and others, and safe hiding places for everything else. Few of us are happy with the amount and kind of storage we now have, and our needs for storage change as we change.

Spend a few minutes analyzing your problem areas. Usually either you do not have the organizing tools you need or you are not efficiently using what you have. It is helpful to visit hardware, office, electronic, scientific, art, or sports supply stores for storage ideas. But don't think you have to store art supplies in $7.98 art bins when a $2.00 fishing tackle box works fine. We have a friend who stores yarn in large drain tiles, food for her vacation home in file cabinets (to keep the mice out), and cleaning supplies in an old hanging shoe bag.

You do not have to go out and spend $400 on ready-made storage units; there are many inexpensive ways to deal with your unique storage needs. Much can be scrounged, bought second-hand at garage sales and thrift shops, purchased from a wholesaler, or obtained from other unlikely sources. For example, to house Tony's comic book collection, we recently bought sturdy cardboard boxes at 22¢ each from a paper dealer.

To help your own ideas along, here is a basic list, by function, of ways to store items:

Hang-Ups

hooks—cup, coat, plastic
nails, tacks, pushpins
angle irons
clothespins and clothesline (perfect for bills)
pegboards
racks (all sizes)—shoe, wine, hat, kitchen utensil
hangers—clips, paper, coat, magnetic
shoe bags (with many pockets)

Shelves

book, record, stereo
industrial metal shelving
dividers—metal, wood, plastic
carousels—lazy Susan, plastic turntables, desk, fullsize (as
    for nails)

Displays

bulletin boards
blackboard
easels—stand and racks, copy holders, recipe holders
bookends—wood, metal, brick
frames—photo, art

Note-Taking

scrap paper—computer, memo
pads (all sizes)
$3 \times 5''$ file cards or larger
notebooks (all sizes)
tape recorders and dictating equipment
pregummed labels
calendars

File Systems

envelopes (all sizes)—business, manila, expandable
folders—manila, expandable
cases and boxes with dividers—paper, metal, wood
recipe and file card boxes
blank bound notebooks—artist, composition
binders—ring, spiral-bound, pocket
dividers—clear plastic, alphabetical, numerical, monthly
notebooks (all sizes)
clipboards
sleeves—plastic for slides, business cards
drawer and closet expanders

Containers

bins—metal, wood, cardboard, wire, plastic

pockets and pouches—fabric, plastic, clay (including photography, fishing, and carpentry pocketed vests)

boxes (all sizes)—wood, cardboard, plastic

barrels and drums

tubes and tiles—cardboard mailing, drain, fiberboard

bags—paper, plastic, fabric (flour, onion, hand-made)

baskets—wire, plastic, fiber

cans (all sizes)

lockers—steel (factory, athletic, mail), wire

pots—metal, clay, wood, vegetable (e.g., gourds)

carts—grocery, mail, food, library

cases—suitcases, photographic slide, fishing tackle, hardware

file cabinets

trays—photographic chemical, stackable, printers', dishpans

jars—glass, clay, beakers, vials

Catalogs

Devoke Company
3788 Fabian Way
Palo Alto, CA 94303
data supply organizers

Edmund Scientific
100 Edscorp Building
Barrington, NJ 08007
low-cost scientific gadgetry.

Fidelity Executive
705 Pennsylvania Avenue South
Minneapolis, MN 55426
carboard files and bins, office equipment

Henniker's
779 Bush Street
San Francisco, CA 94120
unusual organizers for the home

Hertz Furniture Systems Company
220 Fifth Avenue
New York, NY 10001
all kinds of organizing systems

Books

Hennessey, James, and Papanek, Victor. *Nomadic Furniture* and *Nomadic Furniture 2*. 2. New York: Pantheon, 1974, $8.95, $4.95 (684H).

Palmer, Bruce. *Making Children's Furniture and Play Structures*, New York: Workman Publishing, 1974, $3.95 (684P) (concepts useful for adult furniture too).

Liman, Ellen. *The Spacemaker Book*. New York: Viking Press, 1977, $9.95 (q747L).

If you live in a metropolitan area, check the classified section of the telephone directory under: Barrels and drums, Boxes—fiber and corrugated, Clothing—used, Containers, Fiberboard products, Tubing, Salvage, Shelving.

Learn to scrounge shamelessly behind major appliance stores (like refrigerator and washing machine places, including discount stores), motorcycle dealers (they use hardwood in their boxes), liquor stores (the divided corrugated boxes are very sturdy), and office supply stores. Go in the mid-morning, before they have dismantled the boxes for the afternoon trash pick-up.

Bibliography

Dewey Decimal Classification numbers given in parentheses when known. Books already listed in the text are not repeated here.

Ardrey, Robert. *African Genesis*. New York: Atheneum, 1961, $6.95 (573A).

Benedict, Ruth. *Chrysanthemum and the Sword: Patterns of Japanese Culture*. Boston: Houghton Mifflin, 1946.

Birdwhistell, Ray L. *Kinesics and Context*. Philadelphia: University of Pennsylvania Press, 1970.

Bliss, Edwin C. *Getting Things Done, the ABC's of Time Management*. New York: Charles Scribner's Sons, 1976, $6.95.

Browne, Harry. *How I Found Freedom in an Unfree World*. New York: Macmillan, 1973, $7.95 (170B).

Chomsky, Noam. *Language and Mind*. New York: Harcourt Brace and World, 1968.

Cooper, Joseph D. *How To Get More Done in Less Time*. New York: Doubleday, 1962, $5.95 (658C).

DeBono, Edward. *The Five-day Course in Thinking*. New York: Basic Books, Inc., 1967, $5.95 (153D).

DeBono, Edward. *New Think*. New York: Basic Books, Inc., 1967, $6.96 (153D).

DeBono, Edward. *PO: A Device for Successful Thinking*. New York: Simon and Schuster, 1972, $5.95 (153D).

DeGrazia, Sebastian. *Of Time, Work, and Leisure*. New York: Twentieth Century Fund, 1962.

Farmer, Richard N. *Why Nothing Seems To Work Anymore*. Chicago: Henry Regnery, 1977 (309.173F).

Goldfern, Donna. *Everywoman's Guide to Time Management*. Millbrae, CA: Les Femmes, 1977, $3.95.

Hall, Edward T. *Beyond Culture*. New York: Anchor/Doubleday, 1976, $7.95 (301.21H).

Hall, Edward T. *The Hidden Dimension*. New York: Doubleday, 1966, $5.50 (301.3H).

Hall, Edward T. *The Silent Language*, New York: Doubleday, 1959, $5.50 (301.24H).

Hoyt, Wade A. "How to make your car last 20 years," *Esquire Magazine*, January, 1970.

Johnson, Wendell. *People in Quandaries: The Semantics of Personal Adjustment*. New York: Harper and Brothers, 1946.

Jung, Carl G. *The Undiscovered Self*. Boston: Little, Brown and Co., 1957 (153J).

Kerr, Walter. *The Decline of Pleasure*. New York: Simon and Schuster, 1962 (136K).

Lakein, Alan. *How To Get Control of Your Time and Your Life*. New York: Wyden Books, 1973, $6.95 (153L).

Linder, Staffan B. *The Harried Leisure Class*. New York: Columbia University Press, 1970, $12.50 (330.1B).

Mackenzie, R. Alec. *The Time Trap; Managing Your Way Out*. New York: AMACOM, 1972, $9.95.

Maklan, David Mark. *The Four-day Workweek: Blue-Collar Adjustment to a Nonconventional Arrangement of Work and Leisure Time*. New York: Praeger, 1977.

Mehrabian, Albert. *Public Places and Private Spaces; The Psychology of Work, Play and Living Environments*. New York: Basic Books, Inc., 1976, $15.95 (155.9M).

Papanek, Victor, and Hennessey, James. *How Things Don't Work*. New York: Pantheon, 1977 (640P).

Piaget, Jean. *The Child's Conception of Time*. New York: Basic Books, Inc., 1969, $7.95.

Pieper, Josef. *Leisure—The Basis of Culture*. North American Library, 1952, 60¢.

Schumacher, E. F. *Small is Beautiful; Economics as if People Mattered*. New York: Harper & Row, 1973, $2.45 (330S).

Simple Living Collective. *Taking Charge; Personal and Political Change Through Simple Living*. New York: Bantam Books, 1977, $1.95.

Szalai, Alexander (Ed.). *The Use of Time; Daily Activities for Urban and Suburban Populations in Twelve Countries*. The Hague: Mouton & Co., 1972.

Toffler, Alvin. *Future Shock*. New York: Random House/Bantam Books, 1970, $1.95 paper.

INDEX

MORE
SELF-HELP
from
BALLANTINE

16

27 million Americans can't read a bedtime story to a child.

It's because 27 million adults in this country simply can't read.

Functional illiteracy has reached one out of five Americans. It robs them of even the simplest of human pleasures, like reading a fairy tale to a child.

You can change all this by joining the fight against illiteracy.

Call the Coalition for Literacy at toll-free **1-800-228-8813** and volunteer.

Volunteer Against Illiteracy. The only degree you need is a degree of caring.

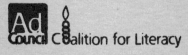

Ad Council   Coalition for Literacy

LV-3